ABOUT THIS BOOK...

This study guide is designed to go with the 2016 Come Fol
page is specifically designed to help you study the importa
found in these valuable lessons.

This book is ideal for anyone! Naturally, leaders and teachers would find this book to
be useful as they prepare to teach. However, the doctrines taught in these lessons
are great study material for anyone and will apply directly to their everyday lives.

Included in these lesson study guides are the following:

- ❖ A variety of ways to record what the scriptures are teaching about each
  subject. Each lesson is designed so that you can study each suggested
  scripture and record the important doctrines and principles and have them all
  in one place so you can easily connect the doctrines taught throughout the
  scriptures.
- ❖ Provided space to study and record suggested General Conference talks and
  other church articles
- ❖ Space to look up and record doctrines and principles found in Church manuals
  and other documents such as *True to the Faith, For the Strength of Youth*, "The
  Family: A Proclamation to the World", "The Living Christ", etc.
- ❖ Specific questions and tips to help you study and understand certain scriptures.
- ❖ Etc.

It is recommended that you keep a *True to the Faith* and a *For the Strength of Youth*
pamphlet nearby as you study. However, everything referenced in this book is found
easily online at Lds.org. For easy access, bookmark the *Come Follow Me* curriculum
site to your toolbar and pull up the individual lessons to find links to each reference.

* Note: This book was updated December 2015. The Come Follow Me Curriculum
may undergo minor changes during 2016. References may be adjusted, talks may be
added or removed, lesson titles may change, or entire lessons may be added or
taken away.

OTHER BOOKS...

Other books offered by this author are some of the following: (visit www.theredheadedhostess.com
for further details, pictures and examples)

- ❖ Book of Mormon Study Guide
- ❖ TOPICS Scripture Study Journal
- ❖ CHAPTERS Scripture Study Journal
- ❖ Seminary Journals
- ❖ Young Women Values Doodle Journal
- ❖ My Scripture Hero Journal
- ❖ Names of Christ Journal
- ❖ And more!

TABLE OF CONTENTS

JANUARY: THE GODHEAD

Young Men/Young Women

Sunday School

FEBRUARY: THE PLAN OF SALVATION

Young Men/Young Women

Sunday School

MARCH: THE ATONEMENT OF JESUS CHRIST

Young Men/Young Women

Sunday School

APRIL: THE APOSTASY AND THE RESTORATION

Young Men/Young Women

Sunday School

TABLE OF CONTENTS SEPTEMBER: COMMANDMENTS

What Do We Know About the Nature of the Godhead?

How do these scriptures help you answer this question?

ARTICLE OF FAITH #1	D&C 130:22

Summarize what you learn about each member of the Godhead in President Boyd K. Packer's talk, "The Witness", General Conference, April 2014.

Heavenly Father	Jesus Christ	The Holy Ghost

How does understanding these truths impact your daily life and choices?

The Godhead

Look up "Godhead" in *True to the Faith*. Record what you learn about the nature of the Godhead here.

OTHER CHRISTIAN BELIEFS

What does Elder Jeffrey R. Holland teach you about what other Christians believe about the Godhead in his talk, "The Only True God and Jesus Christ Whom He Hath Sent", from the October 2007 General Conference?

Look up the following scriptures. As you read them, determine which of the following three doctrines they teach about. Write the scripture references under the correct doctrines.

- Luke 24:39
- Matthew 3:16-17
- John 17:21
- John 14:16
- Acts 7:55-56

- 1 John 5:7
- John 1:14
- 3 Nephi 11:4-11
- Joseph Smith-History 1:17
- D&C 130:22-23

- Alma 11:44
- D&C 20:28
- Article of Faith 1:1
- Genesis 1:26-27

There are three members in the Godhead	The Godhead is united in one	Heavenly Father and Jesus Christ have physical bodies

How did Elder Robert D. Hales gain his testimony of the Godhead? (Read his account in his talk, "Eternal Life---to Know Our Heavenly Father and His Son, Jesus Christ," October 2014 General Conference)

How does having a testimony of the Godhead impact your daily choices and goals?

How did you gain your own testimony of the Godhead?

How Can I Know My Heavenly Father?

What does it take to feel close to your mother and father?

_____

_____

_____

How do those same principles apply to being close to Heavenly Father?

_____

_____

_____

Read John 17:3. What is the difference between knowing *about* someone and *knowing* someone?

_____

_____

_____

What are specific things you can implement better in your life and home to *know* Heavenly Father better?

_____

_____

_____

_____

What has Heavenly Father given us to help us know Him better?

Study the talk, "Seeking to Know God, Our Heavenly Father, and His Son, Jesus Christ," by Elder Robert D. Hales from the October 2009 General Conference. Write down what you learn about what we are given to help us know Heavenly Father. Include your thoughts about how you can implement them better in your life and home.

What do these scriptures teach you about how you can know Heavenly Father?

1 John 2:3-5	
1 John 4:7-8	
Enos 1:1-7	
Mosiah 4:9-12	
Mosiah 5:13	
D&C 88:63-65	
D&C 93:1	

As with any relationship, communicating is important in our relationship with Heavenly Father. What can you learn from these words from Elder Richard G. Scott about improving your communication with God?

What do you learn about knowing your Heavenly Father from Elder Holland's talk, "The Grandeur of God"?

"Using the Supernal Gift of Prayer"
(General Conference, April 2007)

"The Grandeur of God"
(General Conference, October 2003)

Why is Jesus Christ Important in My Life?

Find a copy of "The Living Christ" and use it to find answers to these questions:

Who is Jesus Christ?	What has Christ done for us?	How do we know that Christ lives today?

Study these two talks. Record what they teach you about Jesus Christ and why He is important in your life:

The First Great Commandment	Bear Up Their Burden's with Ease
Elder Jeffrey R. Holland, October 2012 General Conference	Elder David A. Bednar, April 2014 General Conference

WHAT HELP DOES CHRIST OFFER THOSE WHO FOLLOW HIM?

Look up each scripture and write in each box what you learn about the help Christ offers those who follow Him.

John 14:6	John 15:4-5	Mosiah 3:17	Helaman 14:15-18
D&C 18:11-12	D&C 76:41-42	Isaiah 41:10	Isaiah 41:13
Matthew 11:28-30	John 14:27	Philippians 4:13	Mosiah 24:14-15
Alma 7:11-12	Alma 36:3	Alma 36:27	Ether 12:27

WHAT HAS JESUS CHRIST DONE FOR ME?

This is a question that Elder Dallin H. Oaks responded to during a Stake Conference. Read his experience in the talk, "Teachings of Jesus", from the October 2011 General Conference. Then write how he responded about each topic below, using Christ's own words.

Life of the World	Light of the World	Doing the Will of the Father
The Great Exemplar	Priesthood Power	Guidance by the Holy Ghost
Guidance by His Commandments	Focus on Eternal Life	The Atonement

What are the Roles of the Holy Ghost?

Roles of the Holy Ghost

Look up these scriptures and write down what they teach you about the roles of the Holy Ghost.

- John 14:26
- Romans 8:16
- 2 Nephi 32:5
- 1 Kings 19:11-12
- Helaman 5:30
- D&C 85:6
- Galatians 5:22-23
- 3 Nephi 27:20
- Moroni 8:26
- Moroni 10:5
- D&C 42:17
- Moses 1:24

Read "An Unspeakable Gift from God" by Elder Craig C. Christensen's October 2012 General Conference talk. Find the section called, " What Is the Mission of the Holy Ghost?" and write what you learn about the Roles of the Holy Ghost.

_____
_____
_____
_____
_____
_____

What do you learn about the roles of the Holy Ghost from President Boyd K. Packer's talk: "Counsel to Youth" (October 2011 General Conference)?

_____
_____
_____
_____
_____
_____
_____

What does *True to the Faith* teach you about the roles of the Holy Ghost on page 82?

_____
_____
_____
_____
_____
_____
_____
_____
_____
_____
_____
_____
_____
_____
_____
_____
_____
_____

Stories

Look up the following stories about being guided by the Holy Ghost. Summarize each story including notes about whether it would be a good story to share with your family or class.

❖ "Teaching Our Children to Understand" by Cheryl A. Esplin, Ensign, May 2012, pp 10-11. * Find the story about her granddaughter Ashley.

❖ "Only Upon Principles of Righteousness" by Elder Larry Y. Wilson, Ensign, May 2012, pp. 104-105. *Find the story about his daughter.

❖ "The Why of Priesthood Service" by President Dieter F. Uchtdorf, Ensign, May 2012, p. 58. *Find the story about being called as a deacon's quorum president.

Who am I, and who can I become?

What do these scriptures teach you about who you are and who you can become?

Genesis 1:26-27	Psalm 82:6	Moses 1:39	Abraham 3:22-26
Luke 15:4-6	John 3:16	D&C 18:10-15	Luke 15:11-32

Moses

What did Moses learn about himself in Moses 1:4-7?

What did Satan do in verse 12 to confuse Moses? (Notice what he called Moses)

How did Moses handle this situation (verses 13-22)?

What can you learn from Moses in this chapter?

Qualities

Make a list of messages that the world gives about men and women and what qualities are important.

WOMEN	MEN

Go through and highlight or circle all of the false messages written above. What can you do to follow Moses' example when you encounter one of those false messages?

Study one, some, or all of the following General Conference talks. Use these two pages to take notes of what you learn, favorite quotes or phrases and record your personal insights. Leave special notes of stories you may want to use when you teach about this topic.

- ❖ **"Your Happily Ever After"** by President Dieter F. Uchtdorf, April 2010 General Conference
- ❖ **"Living the Gospel Joyful"** by Pres. Dieter F. Uchtdorf, October 2014 General Conference
- ❖ **"The Moral Force of Women"** by Elder D. Todd Christofferson, October 2013 General Conference
- ❖ **"You Can Do It Now"** by President Dieter F. Uchtdorf, October 2013 General Conference
- ❖ **"Four Titles"** by President Dieter F. Uchtdorf, April 2013 General Conference
- ❖ **"Message to the youth from the First Presidency,"** For the Strength of Youth (2011), ii-iii

How does the Holy Ghost help me learn?

In each of the boxes below, record what each scripture teaches you about the role of the Holy Ghost in helping you learn.

John 16:13	*1 Corinthians 2:9-14*	*1 Nephi 10:19*
Alma 5:45-46	*Moroni 10:3-5*	*D&C 11:12-14*

What does President Boyd K. Packer teach you about how the Holy Ghost helps you learn in his talk, "The Quest for Spiritual Knowledge" (New Era, January 2007)?

_____

_____

_____

_____

_____

_____

_____

_____

What 3 things does Brother A. Roger Merrill suggest we do to receive the Spirit? "Receiving by the Spirit", October 2006 General Conference.

1

2

3

Learning By the Holy Ghost

Study this topic in *Preach My Gospel* (page 18) and write what you learn below.

Study, "*Converted to His Gospel through His Church*," by Donald L. Hallstrom, April 2012 Gen. Conf. and write what you learn below.

How can studying the scriptures help me learn about Heavenly Father?

Study Elder D. Todd Christofferson's talk, "The Blessing of Scripture" (General Conference, April 2010) and record on this page what you learn about how studying the scriptures can help you learn about Heavenly Father.

Look up "God" in your Topical Guide and look up some of the scriptures. Write what you learn about Heavenly Father all over this page. Here are some scriptures you could include:

- ❖ Omni 1:17
- ❖ Mosiah 1:3-7
- ❖ Alma 37:8-9
- ❖ D&C 1:37-39
- ❖ D&C 18:34-36
- ❖ Bible Dictionary, "God"

Heavenly Father

How can I help others learn about Heavenly Father?

Record what these 3 books teach you about Heavenly Father:

1. **"God the Father"** (*True to the Faith*, 74-76)
2. **"God is Our Loving Heavenly Father"** (*Preach My Gospel*, 31-32)
3. **"Understanding Those You Teach"** (*Teaching No Greater Call*, 33-34)

Study Alma 30:12-15 and 37-53. Record the reasons Korihor did NOT believe in God, and reasons why Alma DID believe in Him.

Korihor	Alma

Learning from Ammon and Aaron

Study the following scriptures. After you study each group record specific things you can find that Ammon and Aaron did to help Lamoni and his father learn about Heavenly Father.

Alma 18:24-25	
Alma 18:26-28	
Alma 18:29-32	
Alma 18:33-35	
Alma 18:36-37	
Alma 18:38-40	
Alma 22:4-7	
Alma 22:8-11	
Alma 22:12-14	
Alma 22:15-16	
Alma 22:17-19	
Alma 22:20-23	

How can you be like Ammon and Aaron as you teach others about Heavenly Father?

How can I learn to see Heavenly Father's hand in all things?

What do these scriptures teach you about how God is involved in our lives and everything around us?

- ❖ Psalm 145:9
- ❖ 1 Nephi 1:20
- ❖ Alma 30:44
- ❖ Moses 6:63
- ❖ D&C 59:21

O Remember, Remember

Read President Eyring's talk, "O Remember, Remember," from the October 2007 General Conference. Look for the blessings that came to him because he was looking for God's hand in his life. Take your notes here:

The Tender Mercies of the Lord

Read Elder David A. Bednar's talk, "The Tender Mercies of the Lord," from the April 2005 General Conference. Take your notes on this page.

Quick to Observe

Read Elder David A. Bednar's talk, "Quick to Observe," from the December 2006 Ensign. Take your notes on this page about what you learn about seeing Heavenly Father's hand in all things.

How does the Holy Ghost help me teach the Gospel?

Look up the following scriptures and search for answers to the questions below. Write what you learn in the appropriate box.

John 15:26   D&C 11:21   2 Nephi 33:1-2   D&C 50:13-22   Alma 17:3   D&C 52:9   D&C 42:11-17   D&C 84:85

Why is it important to teach by the Spirit?	How does the Spirit bless teachers?
How does the Spirit bless the student?	What should we do to invite the Spirit as we teach?

Teaching and Learning by the Spirit

Read Elder Dallin H. Oak's talk, "Teaching and Learning by the Spirit" from the March 1997 Ensign. Record your notes and insights here:

Teaching after the Manner of the Spirit

Read this talk by Elder Matthew O. Richardson from the October 2011 General Conference. Take your notes here:

Teach By the Spirit

Teaching No Greater Call". 40-48

The Power of the Spirit in Conversion

Look up this topic on pages 92-93 in *Preach My Gospel*. As you read, look for answers to the following question:

What does it mean to teach by the Spirit?

_____

_____

_____

_____

_____

_____

_____

The Student/Investigator

Look up some of the following scriptures. What do they teach you about what the student/investigator needs to feel in order to be taught or converted?

- ❖ 2 Nephi 4:16-35
- ❖ Enos 1
- ❖ Mosiah 4-5
- ❖ Mosiah 18:7-14
- ❖ Mosiah 27-28
- ❖ Alma 5
- ❖ Alma 17-22
- ❖ Alma 32
- ❖ Alma 36
- ❖ Alma 38

The Teacher/Missionary

Look up some of the following scriptures. What do they teach you about what the teacher/missionary needs to do to teach with power?

- ❖ 1 Nephi 8:11-12
- ❖ Mosiah 28:1-4
- ❖ Alma 26
- ❖ Alma 29
- ❖ Alma 31:26-38
- ❖ Alma 32
- ❖ Moroni 7:43-48
- ❖ D&C 4
- ❖ D&C 18:10-16
- ❖ D&C 50:21-22

Sunday School Curriculum

What is the Plan of Salvation?

Label the Plan of Salvation and then look up each of the following scriptures. Determine which part of the Plan each scripture is talking about and record the doctrines taught all over this page. For example, if a scripture is teaching you something about the Pre-mortal life, then write all of the doctrines taught in that scripture next to (or in) the Pre-mortal life on this map.

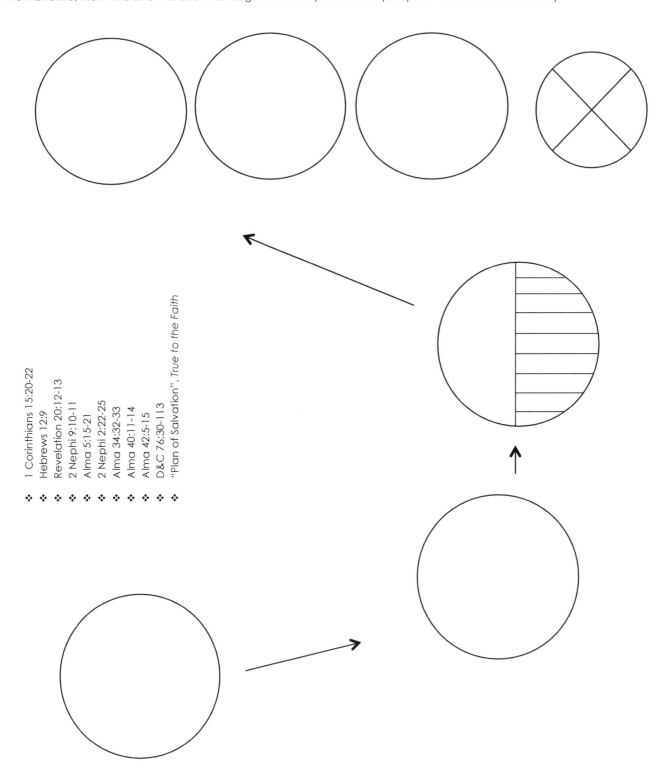

❖ 1 Corinthians 15:20-22
❖ Hebrews 12:9
❖ Revelation 20:12-13
❖ 2 Nephi 9:10-11
❖ Alma 5:15-21
❖ 2 Nephi 2:22-25
❖ Alma 34:32-33
❖ Alma 40:11-14
❖ Alma 42:5-15
❖ D&C 76:30-113
❖ "Plan of Salvation", *True to the Faith*

Study **Alma 12:30** and **Alma 42:5-15.** Look for phrases that are used to describe the Plan of Salvation and write them in this box. What do these phrases teach you about Heavenly Father's plan for His children?

The Race of Life

Find President Thomas S. Monson's talk, "The Race of Life" from the April 2012 General Conference. Take notes about what you learn of the Plan of Salvation here.

A Sure Foundation

Read Elder Dean M. Davies' talk, "A Sure Foundation" from the April 2013 General Conference. Record what you learn about the Plan of Salvation here.

What happened in my premortal life?

Look up these scriptures and references. Record things you learn about the Premortal Life all over this page.

- ❖ "The Influence of Righteous Women" (President Dieter F. Uchtdorf, *Ensign*, Sept 2009)
- ❖ Revelation 12:7-9,11
- ❖ D&C 138:55-56
- ❖ Abraham 3:22-26
- ❖ Moses 4:1-4
- ❖ "Plan of Salvation", *True to the Faith*, pp. 115-17
- ❖ "The Family: A Proclamation to the World"
- ❖ "Pre-Earth Life", *Preach My Gospel*, p. 48

The Premortal Life

What is the purpose of life?

Record in each box what the suggested scripture teaches you about the purpose of life.

2 Nephi 2:25	Alma 12:24	Alma 34:32	Alma 42:4
Abraham 3:25-26	3 Nephi 12:3-12	3 Nephi 12:48	D&C 138:53-56

Read 3 Nephi 12:3-12 and find all of the BEATITUDES that Heavenly Father wants us to develop during our mortality and write them in this box:

Read "The Family: A Proclamation to the World" and find anything that teaches you about your purpose. Write what you find in this box.

Your Happily Ever After"

Read President Dieter F. Uchtdorf's talk, "Your Happily Ever After." Record what you learn about the purpose of life in the left column. In the right column, record personal insights, goals, experiences, etc.

Why do the choices I make matter?

Look up "Agency and Accountability" in *For the Strength of Youth*. Record the phrases that stand out to you.

Choose another standard in *For the Strength of Youth*. Read about that standard and consider the choices you have made in your life as you have strived to live it. Compare your choices to the phrases to the left you have written about "Agency and Accountability". Record your thoughts here:

Record what these scriptures teach you about our choices.

Joshua 24:15	John 14:15	2 Nephi 2:16
2 Nephi 2:27	Helaman 14:30-31	Moroni 7:14-15

Look up some or all of the following talks or articles. Use the next two pages to take notes on what you learn about our choices and why they matter.

❖ "The Three Rs of Choice" by President Thomas S. Monson, October 2010 General Conf.
❖ "Decisions for Eternity" by Elder Russell M. Nelson, October 2013 General Conference
❖ "The Choice Generation," by Randall L. Ridd, April 2014 General Conference.
❖ "Guardians of Virtue" by Sister Elaine S. Dalton, April 2011 General Conference
❖ "Free Forever, to Act for Themselves," D. Todd Christofferson, Oct 2014 General Conference
❖ "Agency," True to the Faith
❖ "Choice and Accountability," *Personal Progress*, 46-49

Why do we have adversity?

Learning from women in the scriptures:

Study these scriptures about times that women faced adversity in the scriptures. What can you learn from them about how we should face adversity?

1 Samuel 1	
1 Kings 17	
Ruth 1	
Esther 4	
1 Nephi 5:1-9	

What do these scriptures teach you about the purpose of adversity and how we can endure it well?

2 Nephi 2:11	
Mosiah 23:21	
Ether 12:27	
D&C 58:3-4	
D&C 121:7-8	
D&C 122:4-9	

Study some or all of the following talks and record what impresses you on these two pages.

- ❖ "Mountains to Climb" by President Henry B. Eyring, April 2012 General Conference
- ❖ "Spiritual Whirlwinds," Elder Neil L. Andersen, April 2014 General Conference
- ❖ "I Will Not Fail Thee, nor Forsake Thee" by President Thomas S. Monson, October 2013 General Conference
- ❖ "Claim the Blessings of Your Covenant" by Sister Linda S. Reeves, October 2013 General Conference
- ❖ "Adversity," True to the Faith

How can I find comfort when someone I care about dies?

What do you think are some common questions, fears, and concerns that people have when someone they care about dies?

Doors of Death

Read the talk "Doors of Death" by Elder Russell M. Nelson from the April 1992 General Conference. Note the things he teaches that give comfort to those suffering a loss of a loved one.

Scriptures

What do these scriptures teach you about death? Notice if any of these scriptures answer any of the questions you wrote above.

Mosiah 18:8-10	Alma 11:42-45	Alma 28:12	D&C 42:45-46	Alma 40:11-14

D&C 137:5-10	1 Corinthians 15:22	D&C 138:57-58	Mosiah 16:7-8	D&C 138

Read one or both of these talks looking for things you can say to someone when they lose someone they love.

- ❖ "Mrs. Patton – the Story Continues" by President Thomas S. Monson, October 2007 General Conference
- ❖ "Because I Live, Ye Shall Live Also" by Elder Shayne M. Bowen, October 2012 General Conference

_____
_____
_____
_____
_____
_____
_____
_____
_____
_____
_____
_____
_____
_____
_____
_____
_____
_____
_____

Why should I treat my body like a temple?

What do these scriptures teach you about the purpose of adversity and how we can endure it well?

1 Corinthians 6:19-20	
D&C 93:33-35	
D&C 88:15-16	
D&C 130:22	
Moses 6:9	

Joseph

What can you learn from Joseph about showing respect for our bodies? **Genesis 39:1-21**

Daniel

What can you learn from Daniel and his friends about showing respect for our bodies? **Daniel 1:3-21**

What are some common lies that Satan uses to try and deceive us from these truths?

For the Strength of Youth

Look through the *For the Strength of Youth* pamphlet and identify every standard that helps us treat our bodies like a temple. Search those standards and find answers to:

why we should treat our bodies like a temple.

Read one or all of these talks looking for things you can learn about the sacredness of our bodies

- ❖ "Great Shall Be the Peace of Thy Children" by President Gordon B. Hinckley, October 2000 General Conference
- ❖ "Ye Are the Temple of God" by Elder David A. Bednar, Ensign, September 2001, p.18
- ❖ "The Sanctity of the Body" Sister Susan W. Tanner, October 2005 General Conference

What is my role in fulfilling Heavenly Father's plan?

Young Men/Duty to God

Search the *Duty to God* book for all of the Priesthood duties (pages 23, 46-47, 70-71); D&C 20:46-60, 75-79; 84:111; 38:42;107:68 and Moses 1:39. Write every action word or phrase in the left column. Then in the right column brainstorm as many ideas you can of ways each of those duties can be fulfilled and magnified.

Priesthood Duties	Ideas

Young Men Curriculum

Why is learning an important part of Heavenly Father's plan?

What principles of learning do these scriptures teach you?

2 Nephi 28:27-30	
D&C 98:11-12	
Alma 12:9-11	
D&C 50:40	
D&C 88:77-80	

Education

Look up "Education" in the *For the Strength of Youth* pamphlet. Read about the standard, including the scriptures. Fill in the columns with the information you find.

Things Heavenly Father wants us to do	Blessings Heavenly Father has promised

Learning and Latter-Day Saints

Read the talk, "Learning and Latter-Day Saints" by Elder and Sister Oaks (*Ensign*, April 2009, 22-27). Take notes on this page.

Why is teaching the gospel important in the plan of salvation?

Who are some teachers who have taught you the gospel in a way that has had an impact in your life? What did they do that made them so memorable to you?

_____

_____

_____

_____

_____

_____

Considering those teachers you wrote about above, how would you answer the question: "Why is teaching an important part of the plan of salvation"?

_____

_____

_____

_____

_____

_____

What do these scriptures teach you about the importance of teaching?

2 Nephi 2:8	D&C 43:8	Luke 2:46-52	D&C 88:77-80

Teaching, No Greater Call

Read pages 3 and 4 in _Teaching No Greater Call_ and look for answers to the question "why is teaching an important part of the plan of salvation?"

_____

_____

_____

_____

_____

What is the role of agency in learning the gospel?

Here are three examples of people who desired and sought learning. Record the principles of learning you learn from each of them.

Nephi 1 Nephi 2:14-16; 11:1	*Joseph F. Smith* D&C 138:1-11	*Joseph Smith* Joseph Smith-History 1: 10-18

What do these scriptures teach you about the question, "What is the role of agency in learning the gospel"?

John 7:17	
D&C 58:26-28	
1 Nephi 10:19	
2 Nephi 2:26	
D&C 50:24	
D&C 88:118	

Seek Learning By Faith

Read the talk "Seek Learning by Faith" by Elder David A. Bednar (*Ensign*, September, 2007, 61-68). Record your favorite quotes, phrases and personal insight here.

How can I help others participate in learning?

On the home page of the Come Follow Me website for the youth curriculum, you can find *Teaching the Gospel in the Savior's Way*. Find the section titled "Teaching the Savior's Way" and write what you learn about each of these principles.

Once you write about the principles, look up the following scriptures and match them to the principles they are exemplifying.

Matthew 16:13-16   Matthew 28:18-19   Luke 10:1-9   Mark 10:17-21   Luke 7:36-43   John 3:1-13

3 Nephi 11:13-15   3 Nephi 17:1-3   D&C 88:122

He loved them	He knew who they were

He prepared himself	He used the scriptures

He shared simple stories, parables and real-life examples	He asked questions

He invited them to testify	He trusted them

He invited them to act in faith	He was their example and mentor

Sunday School Curriculum

Teaching No Greater Call

Look up each of the following topics in Lesson 14 in *Teaching No Greater Call*. Record what you learn along with any insights you have.

Use Questions	
Select teaching methods that relate the discussions to the lessons	
Be sensitive to the Spirit's influence on those present	
Find ways for all to participate	
Maintain the focus of the lessons	
Maintain order	
Do not talk too much	
Do not end discussions too soon	
Listen	
Acknowledge all contributions	
Rescue those who give incorrect answers	
Bring discussions to a close	

Find the section titled "Inviting Children to Act" in Elder David A. Bednar's talk, "Watching with All Perseverance" from the April 2010 General Conference. Record what stands out to you.

How can I use Church music to learn about the plan of salvation?

Read the section "Enhancing Lessons with Music" in *Teaching, No Greater Call* (pages 172-173). Write what you learn about the five ways to use music in teaching.

Record what each of these things teaches you about how to use music:

D&C 25:12	Colossians 3:16
"Music and Dancing" in *For the Strength of Youth*	*"First Presidency Preface" in the Hymn book*

"Worship Through Music," Elder Dallin H. Oaks, October 1994 General Conference

Sunday School Curriculum

How can I help others understand the doctrine of Christ?

2 Nephi 31 teaches about the
doctrine of Christ. On the top half
of this page draw pictures or some
sort of diagram that you could use
to teach others the doctrine in this
chapter.

In this space, record how the
following references help you
answer the question, "How can I
help others understand the
doctrine of Christ?"

2 Nephi 25:26

3 Nephi 11:32-41

3 Nephi 27:13-21

Article of Faith #4

Preach My Gospel: "The Gospel
of Jesus Christ," pages 60-67.

The Doctrine of Christ

Read Elder D. Todd Christofferson's talk, "The Doctrine of Christ" from the April 2012 General Conference. Use this page for your notes and insights.

What is the Atonement of Jesus Christ?

Study Matthew 26 and 27. Use the timeline below to write down the events that occurred in those chapters.

What do these scriptures teach you about the Atonement?

D&C 19:16-19	Matthew 28:1-10
2 Nephi 9:6-26	Alma 7:11-13

Read "Atonement of Jesus Christ" in *True to the Faith*. Record important points here:

_____

_____

_____

_____

_____

_____

_____

_____

_____

_____

_____

_____

_____

_____

_____

_____

_____

_____

_____

_____

_____

Read "The Living Christ: The Testimony of the Apostles," (Ensign, April 2000, 2-3 or *True to the Faith*, 14-21) and find some phrases that teach about Christ and His Atonement. Pick one of the phrases and write your thoughts about it here:

Christ's Last Words

In the left column, write down Christ's final words on the cross. In the right column record what those words teach you about the Atonement.

D&C 19:16-19, Luke 23:34, 39-43, 46 and John 19:26-30

Read these two talks, and use this and the next page to record your notes and thoughts.

❖ "He is Risen" by President Thomas S. Monson, April 2010 General Conference
❖ "Is Faith in the Atonement of Jesus Christ Written in Our Hearts?" by Sister Linda K. Burton, October 2012 General Conference

What does it mean to have faith in Jesus Christ?

What is faith?

Look up "Faith" in *True to the Faith* and use this space to write what you learn.

_____

_____

_____

_____

_____

_____

_____

_____

_____

_____

_____

_____

_____

_____

_____

_____

_____

_____

Faith & Works

Look up James 2:14-20 and draw a diagram that shows the relationship between faith and works.

Examples

What can you learn from the following scriptures about people who acted on their belief in Christ? Fill this page with what you find.

- ❖ James 1: 5-6
- ❖ Alma 32:21, 26-43
- ❖ Moroni 7: 33-41
- ❖ Esther 4-5
- ❖ Mark 5:25-34
- ❖ Hebrews 11:4-9, 17-29
- ❖ 1 Nephi 4
- ❖ Alma 19:16-29
- ❖ Ether 12:11-22
- ❖ Joseph Smith-History 1:11-19

What do you learn about FAITH from these sources?

- ❖ "Faith," Bible Dictionary
- ❖ "Faith- the Choice is Yours," by Bishop Richard C. Edgley, October 2012 General Conference
- ❖ "Faith," Young Women's Personal Progress, 13-20
- ❖ "Go Forward with Faith," *For the Strength of Youth*
- ❖ "Obedience through Our Faithfulness," by Elder L. Tom Perry, April 2014 General Conference
- ❖ "Let Your Faith Show," by Elder Russell M. Nelson, April 2014 General Conference

How can repentance help me every day?

Write down what you learn about repentance from the following places:

"Repentance," *True to the Faith*

"Repentance," *For the Strength of Youth*

What do these scriptures teach you about repentance?

Isaiah 1:18	
Alma 34:15-16	
Alma 36:6-24	
D&C 1:32	
Alma 19:33	
Mosiah 27:35	
D&C 58:42-43	

What do you learn about REPENTANCE from these sources?

❖ "The Divine Gift of Repentance," by Elder D. Todd Christofferson, October 2011 General Conference
❖ "Repent... That I May Heal You," by Elder Neil L. Andersen, October 2009 General Conference
❖ "Virtue," Young Women's Personal Progress, Value Experience 4

_____
_____
_____
_____
_____
_____
_____
_____
_____

Young Men / Young Women Curriculum

What is Grace?

What do these scriptures teach you about GRACE?

EPHESIANS 2:8-9

2 NEPHI 25:23

PHILIPPIANS 4:13

JACOB 4:6-7

MORONI 10:32-33

In John 15:1-10, Christ uses a vine and the branches of the vine to teach about grace. Write what you learn from these verses here:

What do you learn about GRACE in the following places?

Grace, True to the Faith

Grace, Bible Dictionary

Study Elder David A. Bednar's talks, "In the Strength of the Lord", from the October 2004 General Conference as well as his talk, "Bear Up Their Burdens with Ease," from the April 2014 General Conference. Write your notes here:

Young Men / Young Women Curriculum

Why do I need to forgive others?

Forgiveness
Study President Gordon B. Hinckley's talk, "Forgiveness" from the October 2005 General Conference. Take your notes here.

The Merciful Obtain Mercy
Study President Dieter F. Uchtdorf's talk, "The Merciful Obtain Mercy" from the April 2012 General Conference. Take your notes here.

The Parable of the Unmerciful Servant

Study this parable and write down what is happening and all of the principles you can find in each group of scriptures.

Tip	A "TALENT" is a Greek coin worth approximately 6,000 "pence" in today's value . One pence is worth one day's wage. In today's money one talent could be worth $360,000. Ten thousand talents could be worth 3.6 billion dollars. The amount in this parable is meant to be an impossible sum of money to pay back.
Matthew 18:21-24	
Matthew 18:25-26	
Matthew 18:27	
Tip	A single pence was worth one day's labor or about $60 dollars into today's money. One hundred pence would be around $600.
Matthew 18:28	
Matthew 18:29-30	
Matthew 18:31-34	
Matthew 18:35	

What do the following scriptures teach you about forgiveness?

Matthew 5:44	Matthew 6:14-15	Matthew 18:22-23	D&C 64:9-11
Genesis 45:1-7	1 Nephi 7:21	Luke 23:34	

Young Men / Young Women Curriculum

What is the Resurrection?

Study the following chapters. Write everything you learn about the resurrection in each box.

1 Corinthians 15

Alma 40-41

Luke 24

What do you learn about the RESURRECTION from these sources?

- ❖ "The Resurrection of Jesus Christ," by Elder D. Todd Christofferson, April 2014 General Conference
- ❖ "He is Risen!" by President Thomas S. Monson, April 2010 General Conference
- ❖ "Mrs. Patton- the Story Continues" by President Thomas S. Monson, October 2007 General Conference
- ❖ Alma 11:41-45
- ❖ "Resurrection", *True to the Faith*

How can the Atonement help me during my trials?

Scriptures What do these scriptures teach you about how the Atonement can help you during your trials?

MATTHEW 11:28-30	
PHILIPPIANS 4:13	
1 NEPHI 17:3	
HELAMAN 5:12	
D&C 19:23	
D&C 68:6	
MOSIAH 23:21-22	
MOSIAH 24:8-17	
ISAIAH 53:3-5	
ALMA 7:11-13	

What do you learn about **HOW THE ATONEMENT CAN HELP YOU DURING YOUR TRIALS** from these sources?

- ❖ "Personal Peace: The Reward of Righteousness" by Elder Quentin L. Cook, April 2013 General Conference
- ❖ "Fear Not; I Am with Thee," by Sister Jean A. Stevens, April 2014 General Conference
- ❖ "Because I Live, Ye Shall Live Also" by Elder Shayne M. Bowen, October 2012 General Conference
- ❖ "Adversity," True to the Faith

How can I use the words of living prophets and apostles to strengthen my faith in the Atonement of Jesus Christ?

APOSTLE

Look up "Apostle" in the Bible Dictionary. Find phrases that describe the role of an Apostle. Write what you find here.

Review the past General Conference. Record any quotes that help strengthen your faith in the Atonement of Jesus Christ.

OReview some, or all, of the following references. Record on this page phrases that strengthen your faith in the Atonement.

- ❖ "The Living Christ: The Testimony of the Apostles"
- ❖ "The Atonement" by President Boyd K. Packer, October 2012 General Conference
- ❖ "He Lives! All Glory to His Name!" Elder Richard G. Scott, April 2010 General Conference
- ❖ Jacob 7:11-12
- ❖ Mosiah 13:33-35
- ❖ Mosiah 15:11-12
- ❖ D&C 27:12
- ❖ D&C 107:23
- ❖ D&C 76:22-24

What can the scriptures teach me about the Atonement of Jesus Christ?

What are your three favorite scriptures about the Atonement of Jesus Christ?

	Scripture	Why
1		
2		
3		

....

Look up "Jesus Christ, Types of, in Anticipation" in your Topical Guide. Look up 3 of the references that is a similitude of the Atonement. Record what each scripture teaches you about the Atonement of Jesus Christ.

	Scripture	What it teaches about the Atonement
1		
2		
3		

....

And behold, all things have their likeness, and all things are created and made to bear record of me, both things which are temporal, and things which are spiritual; things which are in the heavens above, and things which are on the earth, and things which are in the earth, and things which are under the earth, both above and beneath: all things bear record of me.
(Moses 6:63)

Read the scripture to the left. Think of any time in the scriptures that Christ is compared to things above, on, in, and under the earth. For example, in Mosiah 16:9 Christ is called the Light of the World.

How can the Book of Mormon help me strengthen my faith in the Atonement of Jesus Christ?

What do the following references teach you about the Atonement of Jesus Christ?

The TITLE PAGE of the Book of Mormon

The INTRODUCTION to the Book of Mormon

2 Nephi 25:26

3 Nephi 27:13-14

Find six more scriptures in the Book of Mormon that strengthen your faith in the Atonement of Jesus Christ and write about them.

Sunday School Curriculum

The Book of Mormon: Strengthening Our Faith in Jesus Christ

Read this talk by Elder Neil L. Andersen found in the October 2011 *Ensign*, pages 39-45. Record your thoughts and insights below.

How can relying on the Savior's grace help me become a better teacher?

How does Ether 12:23-29 apply to you as a teacher?

_____

_____

_____

_____

_____

What do the following scriptures teach you about relying on the Savior's grace to become a better teacher?

Jeremiah 1:5-9	
Moses 6:31-34	
1 Corinthians 1:27-31	
D&C 1:19-23	
Jacob 4:7	
Alma 17:9-11	
Alma 29:9	

What do the following references teach you about teaching and relying on the Savior's grace?

"No Greater Call," Teaching No Greater Call, pages 3-4

_____

_____

_____

_____

_____

_____

_____

"In the Strength of the Lord," by Elder David A. Bednar, Ensign, November 2004, 76-78 (first 11 paragraphs)

_____

_____

_____

_____

_____

_____

"Gospel Learning and Teaching," David M. McConkie, October 2010 General Conference

_____

_____

_____

_____

_____

_____

_____

How can I use comparisons to teach others about the Atonement?

Look up "Comparisons" in Teaching, No Greater Call on pages 163-164. Record what you learn about the purpose of using comparisons.

COMPARISONS:

What do these scripture comparisons teach you about the Atonement of Jesus Christ?

Isaiah 1:18	Matthew 11:28-30
Luke 15:11-32	2 Nephi 1:15
Find your own	Find your own

What do the following comparisons teach you about the Atonement of Jesus Christ?

The story about Little Jim in President James E. Faust's talk: "The Atonement: Our Greatest Hope," from the October 2010 General Conference

The story about the tree in Elder Dallin H. Oak's talk: "The Atonement and Faith" found in the April 2010 *Ensign*, pages 30-34

The stories about Jean Valjean and Sara in Elder D. Todd Christofferson's talk: "Redemption" from the April 2013 General Conference

Why was a restoration necessary?

Pull up this lesson on the Come Follow Me website. At the very beginning is a paragraph summarizing the Apostasy and Restoration. Using that paragraph, make a timeline of the events.

Apostasy Look up "Apostasy" in *True to the Faith* and write down what you learn here.

Restoration Look up "Restoration of the Gospel" in *True to the Faith* and write down what you learn here.

Young Men/Young Women Curriculum

What do these scriptures teach you about the Apostasy and Restoration?

Amos 8:11-12	2 Thessalonians 2:1-3	1 Nephi 13:24-29	Joseph Smith-History 1:5-6
Isaiah 29:13-14	Acts 3:20-21	D&C 1:17-23	D&C 1:30

Study Elder Robert D. Hales' talk "Preparations for the Restoration and the Second Coming: My Hand Shall Be Over Thee" from the October 2005 General Conference. Using his talk, answer the questions below.

How was the gospel first established?

_____

_____

_____

_____

_____

_____

_____

What happened after the Savior's resurrection?

_____

_____

_____

_____

_____

_____

_____

_____

_____

_____

What was the first step to the restoration of the Gospel?

What were some of the obstacles to getting the scriptures to people?

What was the Renaissance or re-birth?

Who was John Wycliffe; what did he accomplish; and what was he fighting against?

Who was being inspired during the 1400's?

Who was William Tyndale and what did he accomplish?

What other men helped ignite the Reformation?

What role did King Henry VIII play in the Reformation?

How did Tyndale's translation of the Bible influence Joseph Smith?

Why do we need the Book of Mormon?

Scriptures What do these scriptures teach you about why we need the Book of Mormon?

Ezekiel 37:15-17	
1 Nephi 13:40	
2 Nephi 3:12	
Articles of Faith 1:8	
2 Nephi 25:23	
2 Nephi 25:26	
2 Nephi 33:10-11	
2 Nephi 29:7-11	
D&C 20:8-16	
Book of Mormon Title Page	
Book of Mormon Introduction	

-----"Another Testimony of Jesus Christ" -----

How do these scriptures demonstrate how "Another Testimony of Jesus Christ" is a good subtitle for the Book of Mormon?

- ❖ 1 Nephi 10:4-6
- ❖ Mosiah 3:5-10
- ❖ 3 Nephi 11:7-11

Doctrines Try and fill this box with quotes from the Book of Mormon where doctrines that were lost during the Apostasy were restored through the teachings of the Book of Mormon. So, you want to find doctrines that are not clearly taught in the Bible. Some good scriptures to start with are: 3 Nephi 11:3-11; Moroni 8:4-26; and Alma 34:32-35.

Title Page and Introduction
What does the "Title Page" and "Introduction" in your Book of Mormon teach you about why we need the Book of Mormon?

What are some of your favorite quotes from these talks that help answer the question, "Why do we need the Book of Mormon"?

❖ "A Witness" by President Henry B. Eyring from the October 2011 General Conference
❖ "Safety for the Soul" by Elder Jeffrey R. Holland from the October 2009 General Conference
❖ "The Book of Mormon – a Book from God" by Elder Tad R. Callister from the October 2011 General Conference

How was the Priesthood restored?

What do these scriptures teach you about the restoration of the Priesthood?

D&C 13	D&C 27:12-13
Joseph-Smith History 1:66-72	Article of Faith 1:5

How does Elder Jeffrey R. Holland's talk, "Our Most Distinguishing Feature" from the April 2005 General Conference help you answer these two questions?

How is the Priesthood conferred?

Why is the Priesthood given this way?

Hebrews 5.4

What does this scripture teach you about men who receive the Priesthood?

What was Joseph Smith's role in the Restoration?

What important points do you learn about Joseph Smith in *True to the Faith*?

_____
_____
_____
_____
_____
_____
_____
_____
_____
_____
_____
_____
_____
_____
_____
_____
_____
_____
_____
_____

What important points do you learn about Joseph Smith in the following scriptures?

D&C 76:22-24
_____

D&35:17-18
_____

D&C 135:3
_____
_____
_____

Study Joseph-Smith History 1:1-25 and list every doctrine and principle that we can learn from Joseph's experience. When you are finished, star or highlight the doctrines that were restored to the earth that others did not know at the time.

Joseph-Smith History 1:1-25

What does Elder Lawrence E. Corbridges' talk, "The Prophet Joseph Smith" (October 2015 General Conference) teach you about Joseph Smith?

_____
_____
_____
_____
_____
_____
_____
_____

What does Elder Neil L Andersen's, "Joseph Smith" (October 2014 General Conference) teach you about Joseph Smith?

_____
_____
_____
_____
_____
_____
_____
_____

Young Men/Young Women Curriculum

Why is the First Vision Important?

Blessings What are some blessings that you have been able to experience because of the First Vision?

What other blessings can you find in President Dieter F. Uchtdorf's talk, "The Fruits of the First Vision" from the April 2005 General Conference?

Study the First Vision in Joseph-Smith History 1:7-25. Record everything you learn about the following doctrines and principles.

THE POWER OF PRAYER

RECEIVING REVELATION

SATAN

HEAVENLY FATHER & JESUS CHRIST

Comparing Visions
Study and compare the following visions to each other.

MATTHEW 3:13-17

ACTS 7:54-60

3 NEPHI 11:3-10

JOSEPH-SMITH HISTORY 1:17

What does Joseph Smith's example teach me about learning the gospel?

What principles can you learn from Joseph Smith about learning the gospel in each of these verses?

Joseph-Smith History 1:10-15	
Joseph-Smith History 1:16-20	
Joseph-Smith History 1:21-26	
Joseph-Smith History 1:27-33	
Joseph-Smith History 1:34-40	
Joseph-Smith History 1:41-47	
Joseph-Smith History 1:48-54	
Joseph-Smith History 1:68-71	
Joseph-Smith History 1:72-75	

Joseph Smith's First Prayer

Study the verses in Hymn #26. Find words and phrases that describe Joseph's approach to learning and write them here:

Gaining Knowledge

Write your favorite quotes from chapter 22 of *Teachings of Presidents of the Church: Joseph Smith*, (261-270).

How can I recognize the difference between truth and error?

What do these verses teach you about distinguishing between truth and error? Make a list of steps you find.

Joseph-Smith History 1:8-20

Moroni 7:12-19

What do the last nine paragraphs from President Boyd K. Packer's talk, "These Things I Know" (April 2013 General Conference), teach you about recognizing the difference between truth and error?

What does Elder Neil L. Andersen's talk, "Joseph Smith" (October 2014 General Conference), teach you about recognizing the difference between truth and error?

_____

_____

_____

_____

_____

_____

_____

_____

_____

_____

What does Elder Marcos A. Aidukaitis' talk, "If Ye Lack Wisdom" (April 2014 General Conference), teach you about recognizing the difference between truth and error (the 6th and 7th paragraphs)?

_____

_____

_____

_____

_____

_____

_____

_____

_____

_____

_____

_____

What doctrines and principles do you learn from these scriptures about recognizing the difference between truth and error?

John 8:31-32

Joseph Smith-Matthew 1:37

Isaiah 5:20

Moses 4:3-4

Moroni 10:5

D&C 46:7-8

Why is it important to teach pure doctrine?

Keeping the Doctrine Pure

What stands out to you in Lesson 11, "Keeping the Doctrine Pure" of *Teaching No Greater Call* (Pages 52-53, and 203-207)?

How does the world try to change people's behavior?

How does the Lord influence behavior?

(Alma 4:19 and Alma 31:5)

What does Elder D. Todd Christofferson's talk, "The Doctrine of Christ" (April 2012 General Conference) teach you about the importance of pure doctrine?

_____

_____

_____

_____

_____

_____

_____

Study about some of the people in the scriptures who taught false doctrines. In the second column record the false doctrines they taught. In the third column record how their doctrines impacted others. In the right column record the doctrines that the Prophets taught in response.

	False Doctrines	Impact	Response
SHEREM (Jacob 7)			
KORIHOR (Alma 30)			
ZORAMITES (Alma 31)			

What do these scriptures teach you about the importance of teaching pure doctrine?

2 Timothy 3:1-5

2 Timothy 4:3-4

2 Nephi 9:28-29

Luke 24:32

Joseph Smith-History 1:11-12

Mosiah 18:19

Moroni 10:5

How can I liken the events of the Apostasy and the Restoration to my life?

What was happening in Joseph Smith's life when he was 14 years old? (Joseph-Smith History 1:5-10)

How did Joseph liken the scriptures he read to his life? (Joseph-Smith History 1:11-20)

How can you relate to Joseph? What can you learn from how he likened the scriptures he read to his own life?

What do these scriptures teach you about likening the scriptures to yourselves?

1 Nephi 19:23-24   D&C 61:36

Likening: What strategies can you learn about likening the scriptures in lesson four of *Teaching No Greater Call* (pages 170-171)?

Look up "Apostasy" in *True to the Faith*. In the left column, list the things that led to the Great Apostasy. Then, in the right column liken the events in the left column (that happened on a large scale to many people) to things that could lead someone to personal apostasy today (to one individual, and not a large group).

The Great Apostasy | Personal Apostasy

What teachings can you find in Elder M. Russell Ballard's talk, "Learning the Lessons of the Past" (from the April 2009 General Conference) that would help someone who feels that the scriptures don't relate to them?

_____
_____
_____
_____
_____
_____
_____
_____
_____
_____
_____
_____
_____
_____
_____

How can I explain the Apostasy and the Restoration to others?

Below are scriptures from the Bible that speak of the Apostasy and Restoration of the Gospel. Record what each one teaches about the Apostasy and Restoration.

Isaiah 2:2	
Isaiah 29:14	
Amos 8:11-12	
Acts 3:20-21	
2 Thessalonians 2:1-3	
Ephesians 2:20	

The Only True and Living Church

Read Elder Dallin H. Oak's talk, "The Only True and Living Church" (*New Era*, August 2011, 3-5) and look for what he does to testify of the true Church without offending others.

Bear Testimony Frequently

Study the section "Bear Testimony Frequently" in *Preach My Gospel* on pages 198-199. Make a list of reasons it is important to bear testimony and the guidelines for doing so.

Questions

In the left column, record questions you think that people might have about the Apostasy and the Restoration. Study pages 35-38 in *Preach My Gospel* and record any answers you find to the questions you wrote.

Why is it important to listen to and follow the living prophets?

What counsel have the prophets given to the youth? (Read the "Message from the First Presidency" in *For the Strength of Youth* for some good answers)

What do these scriptures teach you about why we need to listen to and follow the living prophets?

Amos 3:7	D&C 1:4	D&C 1:37-38
Moses 6:26-38	D&C 21:1	D&C 21:4-7

Prophets Read "Prophets" in *True to the Faith* and look for reasons it is important to listen to the Prophets.

Study Elder M. Russell Ballard's talk, "Stay in the Boat and Hold On!" (*Ensign*, May 2012, 126-129). Record what you learn about this talk below.

_____

_____

_____

_____

_____

_____

_____

_____

_____

_____

_____

Study the talk from Carole F. McConkie, "Live according to the Words of the Prophets" (*from the October 2014 General Conference*). Record what you learn about her talk below.

_____

_____

_____

_____

_____

_____

_____

_____

_____

_____

_____

_____

How do I receive personal revelation?

Record several ways you would finish
this sentence:

**I know I am receiving personal
revelation when** _____

PAVILIONS In D&C 121:1-4 Joseph Smith uses a pavilion to illustrate how he was
feeling. What does the pavilion represent in those verses? (Use the
section heading for context)

What do you learn about "pavilions" and "receiving revelation" in President Henry B. Eyring's talk, "Where Is the Pavilion"
(October 2012 General Conference)?

What are some things that might create a pavilion between us and Heavenly Father?

How can we remove these pavilions?

What do these scriptures teach you about receiving revelation and communicating with the Holy Ghost?

1 Kings 19:9-12	Helaman 5:30	D&C 6:14-16	D&C 6:23
D&C 8:2-3	D&C 11:12-14	John 14:26-27	D&C 9:7-9

The Brother of Jared

Study Ether 2-3 and record any insights you gain from the Brother of Jared's experience regarding receiving personal revelation.

PREPARING OURSELVES

What are some ways we can prepare ourselves to receive revelation? (See 3 Nephi 17:2-3 and D&C 9:7-8 for some ideas)

The Spirit of Revelation

What do you learn about receiving revelation from Elder David A. Bednar's talk, "The Spirit of Revelation" (April 2011 General Conference)?

Preach My Gospel What do you learn about receiving revelation from Preach My Gospel (the section titled, "Learn to Recognize the Promptings of the Spirit" on pages 96-97)?

REVELATION
Look up "Revelation" in *True to the Faith* and record what you learn here.

Young Men / Young Women Curriculum

How can I make my prayers more meaningful?

What are some important principles of communication when communicating with others? (Make a list here)

What are some important principles of communicating with Heavenly Father through prayer?

Principles of Prayer
What principles of prayer can you find in these scriptures?

LUKE 22:41-42

HELAMAN 10:5

D&C 46:30-31

----

3 NEPHI 14:7

D&C 9:7-8

MORONI 10:3-5

----

3 NEPHI 17-19

What can you learn from Elder David A. Bednar in these two talks about how to make your prayers more meaningful?

- ❖ "Ask in Faith," April 2008 General Conference
- ❖ "Pray Always," October 2008 General Conference

Young Men / Young Women Curriculum

Prayer

What can you learn from *True to the Faith* and the *Bible Dictionary* about how to make your prayers more meaningful?

_____
_____
_____
_____
_____
_____
_____
_____
_____
_____
_____
_____
_____
_____
_____
_____
_____
_____
_____
_____
_____
_____
_____
_____
_____
_____
_____
_____

Why is it important to study the scriptures?

What do these scriptures teach you about the importance of scripture study?

2 TIMOTHY 3:16-17 →

2 NEPHI 32:3 →

....

The Power of Scripture

Study Elder Richard G. Scott's talk, "The Power of Scripture" from the October 2011 General Conference. Take notes on what most stands out to you as well as the scriptures that have guided his life.

_____

_____

_____

_____

_____

_____

_____

_____

_____

_____

_____

_____

_____

_____

_____

_____

_____

_____

_____

What are some scriptures that have guided your life?

THE IMPORTANCE OF DAILY SCRIPTURE STUDY

What do you learn about the importance of scripture study in *True to the Faith*? (Pages 155-159, "Scriptures")

What do these scriptures teach you about the power of scripture study?

PSALMS 119:105	1 NEPHI 15:24-25	ALMA 31:5	HELAMAN 3:29-30
HELAMAN 15:7-8	D&C 11:21	D&C 84:45	JOSEPH SMITH-MATTHEW 1:37

THE KEY TO SPIRITUAL PROTECTION

What does President Boyd K. Packer's talk teach you about the importance of scripture study? ("The Key to Spiritual Protection," October 2013 General Conference)

Young Men / Young Women Curriculum

How can I strengthen my testimony?

Testimony What do you learn about "testimony" in *True to the Faith*?

Study Alma 32:27-34 and compare how a testimony is like growing a plant.

What do these people teach you about gaining a testimony?

Nephi
1 Nephi 10:17-19

Alma the Younger
Alma 5:45-46

On the left, make a list of things that weaken our testimonies. On the right, make a list of things that strengthen our testimonies. Use the scriptures below for help.

JOHN 7:16-17   1 CORINTHIANS 2:9-13   D&C 8:2-3   JAMES 1:5   1 NEPHI 15:11   3 NEPHI 18:20
                        MORONI 10:3-5 MOSIAH 26:3   ALMA 12:11   D&C 9:7-9

Weaken	*Strengthen*

Study the following talks and find your favorite quotes about strengthening testimonies and record them here:

- ❖ "Believe, Obey, and Endure" by President Thomas S. Monson, April 2012 General Conference (paragraphs 12 and 13)
- ❖ "Receiving a Testimony of Light and Truth," by President Dieter F. Uchtdorf, October 2014 General Conference
- ❖ "Be Ye Converted" by Sister Bonnie L. Oscarson, October 2013 General Conference
- ❖ "I Know These Things of Myself," by Craig C. Christensen, October 2014 General Conference

_____

_____

_____

_____

_____

_____

_____

_____

_____

_____

_____

Young Men / Young Women Curriculum

How can a patriarchal blessing help me?

How has your patriarchal blessing helped you in your life?

_____

_____

_____

_____

_____

_____

_____

_____

What do you learn about "Patriarchal Blessings" in *True to the Faith*?

What principles can you learn in these scriptures that apply to patriarchal blessings?

Alma 16:16-17

3 Nephi 17:2-3

3 Nephi 20:25-27

D&C 82:10

D&C 130:20-21

About Patriarchal Blessings

Look up "About Patriarchal Blessings" in the March 2004 New Era, and answer these questions.

What is a patriarchal blessing?

_____
_____
_____
_____
_____
_____
_____

Why is lineage important?

_____
_____
_____
_____
_____
_____
_____

Who may give a patriarchal blessing?

_____
_____
_____
_____

Who may receive a patriarchal blessing?

_____

How old do I have to be for a blessing?

_____
_____

How is the blessing given?

_____
_____
_____

How do I get a patriarchal blessing?

_____
_____

How can I prepare and what should I wear?

_____

How do I know if I am ready?

_____

Will all the promises in my blessing be fulfilled?

_____
_____

When will the promises in my blessing be fulfilled?

_____
_____
_____

Should I let others read my blessing?

_____
_____

What do you learn about "Patriarchal Blessings" in *these two talks?*

- ❖ "You Have a Noble Birthright," by Sister Julie B. Beck (Ensign, May 2006, 106-108)
- ❖ "Help Them Aim High," by President Henry B. Eyring (October 2012 General Conference)

What can I learn from living prophets and apostles?

What do these scriptures teach you about the importance of prophets and apostles?

Mosiah 8:16-18	D&C 1:38	D&C 68:3-4

Study the talk, "General Conference: Strengthening Faith and Testimony," by Elder Robert D. Hales (October 2013 General Conference) and look for what we can do to receive the most from General Conference.

_____

_____

_____

_____

_____

_____

_____

_____

_____

_____

_____

_____

_____

_____

_____

_____

_____

_____

_____

_____

PROPHETS

What can you learn from *True to the Faith* about "Prophets" that will help you answer the question, "What can I learn from prophets and apostles"?

What do you learn about the importance of listening to prophets and apostles in *these two talks?*

- ❖ "An Ensign to the Nations" by Elder Jeffrey R. Holland (April 2011 General Conference)
- ❖ "These Things I Know" by President Boyd K. Packer (April 2013 General Conference)

_____
_____
_____
_____
_____
_____
_____
_____
_____
_____
_____
_____
_____
_____
_____
_____
_____
_____
_____

Feast upon the words of Christ

What do you think it means to truly "feast upon the words of Christ" (2 Nephi 32:3)?

_____

_____

What does Elder David A. Bednar's talk, "A Reservoir of Living Water," (CES Fireside for Young Adults [February 4, 2007]) teach you about how you can improve your scripture study?

_____

_____

_____

_____

Look up the following scriptures and look for what they teach you about the following 3 important principles of scripture study. Record what you learn under each principle.

Isaiah 34:16   **1 Nephi 19:23**   **D&C 138:1-11**   **1 Nephi 10:19**   **Psalm 119:105**   **D&C 88:63**   **2 Nephi 4:15-16**
               D&C 88:118   **Joseph-Smith History 1:11-13**   **D&C 11:22**   **Joseph-Smith Matthew 1:37**

Search	Ponder	Pray

MAY: PROPHETS AND REVELATION

A Discussion on Scripture Study

Study this talk by President Eyring from the July 2005 Ensign. Take notes under each question.

How has scripture study benefited you personally?

Why should we read the Book of Mormon on an ongoing basis?

What have you done to make your own scripture study more meaningful?

How can Latter-day Saints make scripture study a priority?

What roles do fasting and prayer play in scripture study?

How can parents help their children love the scriptures?

How can seminary help young people learn to love the scriptures?

Why is it important to teach the approved curriculum?

What is the role of the Holy Ghost in scripture study?

What can we look forward to as we consistently study the scriptures?

Read about each of these study aids and how they can help you improve your scripture study in *Teaching, No Greater Call* (pages 56-59, 137-138)

Bible Dictionary

Footnotes & Cross-References

Headings of Chapters & Sections

Introductory Pages

Maps

Topical Guide

How does reverence help me receive revelation?

REVERENCE
Study "Reverence" and "Revelation" in *True to the Faith* and record what you learn.

To Hold Sacred
Study the talk, "To Hold Sacred" by Elder Paul B. Pieper from the April 2012 General Conference. Record your favorite quotes and personal thoughts.

What do these scriptures teach you about the relationship between reverence and revelation?

1 Kings 19:12

3 Nephi 11:1-7

Psalm 46:10

D&C 63:64

D&C 84:54-57

Reverence Invites Revelation

Study the talk, "Reverence Invites Revelation" by President Boyd K. Packer from the October 1991 General Conference. Record your favorite quotes and personal thoughts.

_____

_____

_____

_____

_____

_____

_____

_____

_____

_____

_____

_____

_____

_____

_____

_____

_____

_____

What does it mean to bear testimony?

Look up this lesson on the Come Follow Me website. Read the first paragraph and answer the following questions.

What is a testimony?

What do we do when we bear testimony?

What is the foundation of a testimony?

What do you learn about what a testimony is in the section called, "What is a Testimony?" *in Teaching No Greater Call* (pages 43-44)?

Examples in the Scriptures:

Here are some examples in the scriptures of people bearing testimony. Record your observations about each testimony.

MATTHEW 16:13-19	MOSIAH 3:17	ALMA 5:45-48
ALMA 7:13	D&C 76:22-24	ALMA 4:18-20
ALMA 11:39-41	ALMA 12:1	ALMA 15:12

What do the following talks and articles teach you about bearing testimony?

❖ "Witnesses for God" by President Henry B. Eyring, from the October 1996 General Conference
❖ "The Power of a Personal Testimony" by President Dieter F. Uchtdorf from the October 2006 General Conference
❖ "Testimony" by Elder Dallin H. Oaks from the April 2008 General Conference
❖ "Bear Testimony Frequently" from *Preach My Gospel* 198-199

What can I learn from President Monson about following the Spirit?

What do these scriptures teach you about following the promptings of the Spirit?

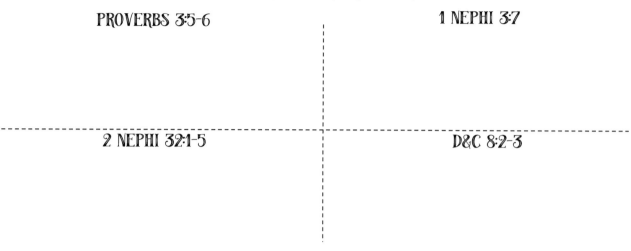

PROVERBS 3:5-6

1 NEPHI 3:7

2 NEPHI 32:1-5

D&C 8:2-3

Read the following stories/talks by President Monson where he teaches about following the Spirit. Record what you learn from him in each story.

1 "Consider the Blessings" from the October 2012 General Conference

2 "Stand in Holy Places" from the October 2011 General Conference (the story about the dedication of the Frankfurt temple).

3 "Tabernacle Memories" from the April 2007 General Conference (the story about the girl in the balcony).

What can you learn about President Monson from Elder Jeffrey R. Holland's article, "President Thomas S. Monson: In the Footsteps of the Master" in the June 2008 *Ensign*, pages 2-16?

What is the Priesthood?

Look up this lesson on the Come Follow Me website. Read the first paragraph and answer the following questions.

What is the Priesthood?

What are some reasons why Heavenly Father uses the Priesthood?

What is the foundation of a testimony?

Scriptures: What do you learn about the Priesthood from these scriptures?

Hebrews 5:4

D&C 42:11

Article of Faith #5

Alma 13:1

D&C 107:1-5

D&C 84:17-22

D&C 121:34-46 What principles are central to power in the Priesthood?

True to the Faith
Look up the following things in *True to the Faith* and record what you learn.

Priesthood (pages 124-128)

Aaronic Priesthood (pages 3-4)

Melchizedek Priesthood (pages 101-2)

What do the following talks teach you about the Priesthood?

- ❖ "This is My Work and My Glory" by Elder M. Russell Ballard (April 2013 General Conference)
- ❖ "Power in the Priesthood," by Elder Neil L. Andersen (October 2013 General Conference)

What are my responsibilities in the work of the priesthood?

YOUNG WOMEN THEME

D&C 20:38-60 What connections do you see between the duties of priesthood holders listed in these verses and the Young Women Theme?

"THE KEYS AND AUTHORITY OF THE PRIESTHOOD"

Read section IV in Elder Dallin H. Oak's talk, "The Keys and Authority of the Priesthood" (April 2014 General Conference). What do you learn about the priesthood and how it applies to women?

FEMALE DISCIPLES

Study chapter one in *Daughters in My Kingdom: The History and Work of Relief Society*. Record your thoughts about female disciples and how they assist in the work of the Priesthood.

What do these scriptures teach you about the power of a righteous woman?

Alma 56:47-48

Alma 57:21

Moses 5:11-12

D&C 25:6-8

What are the keys of the Priesthood?

Look up this lesson on the Come Follow Me website. Read the first paragraph and answer the following questions.

What are priesthood keys?

Who holds all of the keys to lead the Church?

Who else holds priesthood keys?

What do you learn about "Priesthood Keys" in *True to the Faith* (pages 126-127)?

What do these scriptures teach you about the keys of the Priesthood?

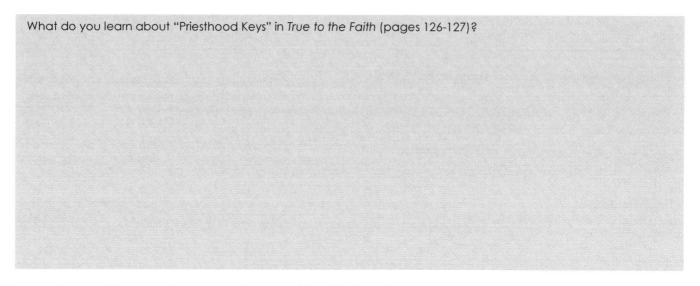

Matthew 16:18-19	Mosiah 25:19	D&C 65:2
D&C 124:123	D&C 124:142-143	D&C 132:7

What do the following talks teach you about keys of the Priesthood?

- ❖ "The Twelve" by President Boyd K. Packer (April 2008 General Conference)
- ❖ "Keys of the Priesthood" by Elder Russell M. Nelson (October 1987 General Conference)
- ❖ "The Keys and Authority of the Priesthood" by Elder Dallin H. Oaks (April 2014 General Conference)

Young Men/Young Women Curriculum

How do I receive the power and blessings of the priesthood in my life?

Look up this lesson on the Come Follow Me website. Read the first paragraph and answer the following question:

What can we receive because of the Priesthood?

What do the following scripture stories teach you about how the Priesthood can bless us?

John the Baptist

Matthew 3:1-6, 13-17

Peter & John

Acts 3:1-10

Alma

Mosiah 18:7-18

Jesus Christ

3 Nephi 18:1-5

What do you learn in the book *Daughters in My Kingdom: The History and Work of Relief Society* in the chapter, "Blessings of the Priesthood for All: An Inseparable Connection with the Priesthood (pages 127-133).

What do the following talks teach you about the blessings of the Priesthood?

- ❖ "Priesthood Authority in the Family and the Church" by Elder Dallin H. Oaks (October 2005 General Conference)
- ❖ "Do We Know What We Have?" by Sister Carole M. Stephens (October 2013 General Conference)
- ❖ "Power in the Priesthood" by Elder Neil L. Andersen (October 2013 General Conference)

What does it mean to sustain my Church leaders?

Honor and Uphold
What does it mean to honor and uphold something?

Exodus 17:8-12
How does this story relate to us as we sustain our Priesthood leaders?

Blessings & Warnings
What blessings and warnings do these scriptures give for those who do (or don't) honor the Priesthood?

D&C 124:45-46

D&C 21:1-6

Article of Faith #5

Why is it important to understand and have a testimony of this Article of Faith?

_____

_____

_____

_____

_____

Did not honor and uphold

What can you learn from these people who rejected the Priesthood?

Saul	**Laman & Lemuel**	**Children of Israel**
1 Samuel 15:1-28	1 Nephi 18:8-20	D&C 84:23-25

Did honor and uphold

What can you learn from these people who honored and upheld the Priesthood?

The Widow of Zarephath	**Naaman**	**The Nephites**
1 Kings 17:8-16	2 Kings 5:1-14	3 Nephi 9:10-15

What do the following talks teach you about honoring and upholding the Priesthood?

- ❖ "Called by God and Sustained by the People" by President Henry B. Eyring (*Ensign*, June 2012, 4-5)
- ❖ "Called and Chosen" by President James E. Faust (October 2005 General Conference)

How can I participate effectively in councils in the Church?

Look up this lesson on the Come Follow Me website. Read the first paragraph and answer the following questions:

What is the purpose of Church councils?

What makes councils effective?

What can we learn to do to participate effectively in council meetings?

What doctrines and principles can you learn from these scriptures to understand the purpose of councils and participate effectively?

Matthew 18:20   Moroni 6:4-5

D&C 38:27   D&C 88:122

Participating Effectively   As you are studying this lesson, fill this box with characteristics that would make someone effective as they participate in Church councils.

Sunday School Curriculum

What do the following talks teach you about Church councils?

❖ "Learning in the Priesthood" by President Henry B. Eyring (April 2011 General Conference)
❖ "Acting on the Truths of the Gospel of Jesus Christ" by President Dieter F. Uchtdorf (Worldwide Leadership Training Meeting, February 2012)

How do women and priesthood holders work together to build the Kingdom of God?

Study "The Family: A Proclamation to the World" and identify specific ways that men and women work together to build the Kingdom of God.

What do the following talks or articles teach you about women and the priesthood working together?

❖ Chapter 8 of *Daughters in My Kingdom: The History and Work of Relief Society*, "Blessings of the Priesthood for All: An Inseparable Connection with the Priesthood" (pages 125-143)
❖ "LDS Women are Incredible!" by Elder Quentin L. Cook (April 2011 General Conference)

Why is it important to follow the counsel given by priesthood leaders?

What can you learn from these people in the scriptures who followed the counsel of a priesthood leader?

Naaman	Sons of Mosiah	Zoram
2 Kings 5:1-14	Mosiah 28:1-8	Alma 16:5-8

Use these scriptures to help you answer the question, "Why is it important to follow the counsel given by priesthood leaders?"

Ephesians 4:11-14

D&C 1:38

D&C 21:4-5

D&C 124:45-46

What do you learn from this talk about following the counsel of our priesthood leaders?

❖   "Two Lines of Communication" by Elder Dallin H. Oaks (October 2010 General Conference)

How can using scripture study skills help me learn more about the priesthood?

Study the following scriptures about the priesthood. In the center column, look up and write the definitions of words you do not know. In the right column, write what you learn about the priesthood from that scripture.

Reference	Definitions	What I learned about the priesthood
D&C 121:34-35		
D&C 121:36-37		
D&C 121:38-39		
D&C 121:40-41		
D&C 121:42-43		
D&C 121:44-45		
D&C 121:46		

Look up "Melchizedek Priesthood" in the Bible Dictionary. Look up the suggested scriptures and write what you learn all around the "Melchizedek Priesthood" below.

Melchizedek Priesthood

Study the following scriptures about the priesthood. In each box write what you learn about the priesthood. Include definitions and what you learn from the footnotes in each verse.

D&C 20:46	D&C 20:47	D&C 20:48	D&C 20:49-50
D&C 20:51	D&C 20:52	D&C 20:53	D&C 20:54
D&C 20:55-56	D&C 20:57	D&C 20:58	D&C 20:59
D&C 84:33	D&C 84:34	D&C 84:35	D&C 84:36
D&C 84:37	D&C 84:38	D&C 84:39	D&C 84:40
D&C 84:41	D&C 84:42	D&C 84:43	D&C 84:44

How can I use stories to teach others about the priesthood?

Look up this lesson on the Come Follow Me website. Read the first paragraph and answer the following question:

Why are stories powerful teaching tools?

Read about "Stories" in *Teaching, No Greater Call* (pages 179-182). Write down what you learn in this box.

Here are four scripture stories about the priesthood. Study the stories and write a summary of what they are about in the center column. In the right column write down specific doctrines and principles that story teaches.

Acts 3:1-9		
Acts 8:14-24		
3 Nephi 18:1-9		
Luke 10:1		

What meaningful stories can you find in the following talks? What doctrines and principles do they teach?

- ❖ "On Being Genuine," by President Dieter F. Uchtdorf (April 2015 General Conference)
- ❖ "The Powers of Heaven" by Elder David A. Bednar (April 2012 General Conference)
- ❖ "The Priesthood of Aaron" by Elder L. Tom Perry (October 2010 General Conference)

Why are ordinances important in my life?

Look up this lesson on the Come Follow Me website. Read the first paragraph and answer the following questions:

What is an ordinance?

Who performs ordinances?

What is the purpose of ordinances?

Ordinances Look up "Ordinances" in *True to the Faith* and write what you learn in this box.

Requirements Look up and write about the four requirements for performing ordinances in Handbook 2: Administering in the Church ("Priesthood Ordinances and Blessings", section 20.1). In the right column, look up 3 Nephi 11:21-26 and write how each requirement is met in the Savior's description of baptism.

1

2

3

4

Baptism Record everything you learn about baptism in these scriptures. Include requirements, instructions, etc.

Matthew 3:13-17

Acts 19:1-6

3 Nephi 11:21-26

Moroni 8:10-12

What can you learn about ordinances from these talks?

- ❖ "Therefore They Hushed Their Fears," by Elder David A. Bednar (April 2015 General Conference)
- ❖ "An Outpouring of Blessings" by Sister Julie B. Beck (April 2006 General Conference)

Why are covenants important in my life?

Look up this lesson on the Come Follow Me website. Read the first paragraph and answer the following questions:

When do we make covenants?

What is a covenant?

What blessings come from covenants?

Covenant Look up "Covenant" in *True to the Faith* and write what you learn in this box.

People of Ammon What can we learn from the people of Ammon about the importance of keeping our covenants? (Alma 53:10-18 and 56:5-8)

Covenants

What promised blessings can you find in these scriptures for those who make and keep their covenants?

Exodus 19:5	D&C 35:24
D&C 90:24	D&C 82:10

What can you learn about covenants from these talks?

- ❖ "Covenant Daughters of God," by Sister Jean A. Stevens (October 2014 General Conference)
- ❖ "Daughters in the Covenant" by President Henry B. Eyring (April 2014 General Conference)
- ❖ "Keeping Covenants Protects Us, Prepares Us, and Empowers Us" by Sister Rosemary M. Wixom (April 2014 General Conference)

What covenants did I make at baptism?

Your Baptismal Covenant Look up "Baptism" in *True to the Faith*. Find the section titled "Your Baptismal Covenant" and record what you learn about the following things.

Taking upon yourself the name of Jesus Christ

Keeping the Commandments

Serving the Lord

Commitments What commitments do these scriptures teach that we make at baptism?

Mosiah 18:8-10

D&C 20:37

What are some examples of the Savior keeping these commitments during His life?

_____

_____

_____

_____

_____

What do these scriptures teach you about the importance of baptism?

John 3:5

2 Nephi 31:4-13

2 Nephi 31:17

What can you learn about our baptismal covenant from these talks?

- ❖ "The Covenant of Baptism: To Be in the Kingdom and of the Kingdom" by Elder Robert D. Hales (October 2000 General Conference)
- ❖ "We Have Great Reason to Rejoice" by Sister Carole M. Stephens (October 2013 General Conference)

How do I receive the gift of the Holy Ghost?

Look up 1 Nephi 2:9-20 and 1 Nephi 15:1-11. Consider what Nephi did to receive the Holy Ghost and what Laman and Lemuel did to reject it. Record what you find below.

Nephi	Laman and Lemuel

THE LIAHONA

Study 1 Nephi 16:14-29, 1 Nephi 18:8-22 and Alma 37:38-46. Write your thoughts about how the Holy Ghost is like the Liahona.

_____
_____
_____
_____
_____
_____
_____
_____

What do these scriptures teach you about receiving the gift of the Holy Ghost?

ACTS 8:14-17

D&C 33:15

ARTICLE OF FAITH #4

D&C 20:77

D&C 121:45-46

The Gift of the Holy Ghost

Look up "The Gift of the Holy Ghost" in *True to the Faith* and write what you learn in this box.

What can you learn about the Holy Ghost from these talks?

- ❖ "Receive the Holy Ghost" by Elder David A. Bednar (October 2010 General Conference)
- ❖ "That We May Always Have His Spirit to Be with Us" by Elder David A. Bednar (April 2006 General Conference)

Why are temple ordinances important?

Ordinances for the Living

Look up "Temples" in *True to the Faith* and study the section "Ordinances for the Living". Record what you learn in this box.

Temple Marriage

What do you learn about temple marriage in D&C 131:1-4 and D&C 84:19-22?

What do you learn about temple ordinances in these talks?

- ❖ "Blessings of the Temple," by President Thomas S. Monson (April 2015 General Conference)
- ❖ "Roots and Branches" by Elder Quentin L. Cook (April 2014 General Conference)
- ❖ "Temple Worship The Source of Strength and Power in Times of Need" by Elder Richard G. Scott (April 2009 General Conference)

What does it mean to take upon myself the name of Jesus Christ?

Look up this lesson on the Come Follow Me website. Read the first paragraph and answer the following questions:

When do we take upon ourselves the name of Jesus Christ?

How do we fulfill this covenant?

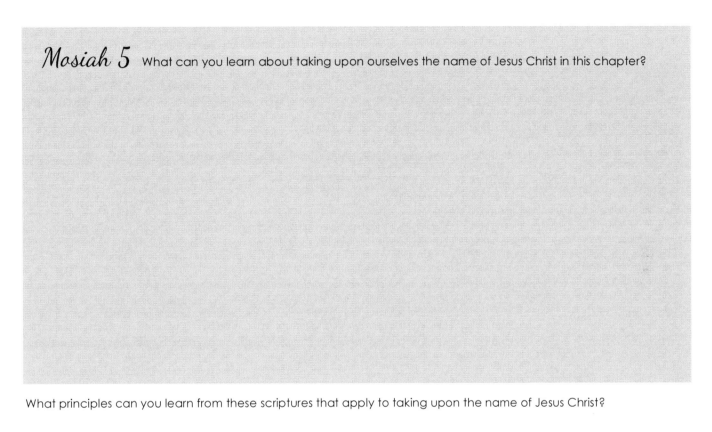

Mosiah 5 What can you learn about taking upon ourselves the name of Jesus Christ in this chapter?

What principles can you learn from these scriptures that apply to taking upon the name of Jesus Christ?

Helaman 5:6-8

3 Nephi 27:27

D&C 20:37, 77

Mosiah 18:9

What do you learn about taking upon the name of Jesus Christ from these talks?

❖ "Being a More Christian Christian" by Elder Robert D. Hales (October 2012 General Conference)
❖ "What Have You Done with My Name?" by Elder Mervyn B. Arnold (October 2010 General Conference)

What spiritual truths can I learn from the ordinances of the Gospel?

What can these ordinances teach you about the Atonement?

Study the scriptures and consider the symbolism of each ordinance and write your thoughts about how they teach you about the Atonement.

Baptism	The Sacrament
Romans 6:3-6 and D&C 76:51	Luke 22:19-20 and 3 Nephi 18:1-11

Remembering the Savior and His Atonement

Look up "Sacrament" in *True to the Faith* and read the section titled "Remembering the Savior and His Atonement" and record what you learn in this box.

Why does the Lord teach us through symbols?

Look up "Comparisons and Object Lessons" in *Teaching, No Greater Call* (pages 163-164). Look for reasons the Lord teaches us through symbols.

JULY: ORDINANCES AND COVENANTS

What do you learn from these references about the spiritual truths in the ordinances of the gospel?

- ❖ "The Holy Temple" by President Boyd K. Packer, *Ensign*, October 2010, 29-35
- ❖ "Ordinances and Covenants" by Dennis B. Neuenschwander, *Ensign*, August 2001, 20-26
- ❖ D&C 84:19-22
- ❖ "Ordinances" *True to the Faith*

How can I deepen my understanding of covenants?

Study about each of the following covenants and write everything you learn below. Included are suggested references. For additional ones, see your *Bible Dictionary*, *Topical Guide* and *Preach My Gospel*.

Abrahamic Covenant   (Abraham 2:8-11, "Abrahamic Covenant" *True to the Faith*)

Baptismal Covenant   (Mosiah 18:8-10 and D&C 20:37, "Baptism" *True to the Faith*)

The Sacrament   (D&C 20:77,79, "Sacrament", *True to the Faith*)

Oath & Covenant of the Priesthood (D&C 84:33-44, "Melchizedek Priesthood", *True to the Faith*)

The Endowment ("Temples, Ordinances for the Living", *True to the Faith*, 171)

Temple Marriage ("The New and Everlasting Covenant of Marriage", *True to the Faith*, 98)

How can I make the sacrament more meaningful to me?

Look up this lesson on the Come Follow Me website. Read the first paragraph and answer the following questions:

What should we do during the sacrament each week?

How do we know if we are worthy to take the sacrament?

The Sacrament   Study Matthew 26:17-30 and imagine what it would have been like to be there. Write your thoughts below.

_____

_____

_____

_____

_____

_____

_____

_____

Now study 3 Nephi 18:1-13. What would it have been like to be there? What would have been some similarities and differences from the event in the book of Matthew you just wrote about?

_____

_____

_____

_____

_____

_____

_____

_____

_____

_____

_____

_____

What can I learn from these scriptures on how to prepare for the sacrament?

1 CORINTHIANS 11:23-29	3 NEPHI 9:20
D&C 20:37	D&C 59:8-12

What do you learn from these three talks about how you can make the sacrament more meaningful?

- ❖ "Sacrament Meeting and the Sacrament" by Elder Dallin H. Oaks (October 2008 General Conference)
- ❖ "Coming to Ourselves: The Sacrament, the Temple, and Sacrifice in Service" by Elder Robert D. Hales (April 2012 General Conference)
- ❖ "Blessings of the Sacrament" by Elder Don R. Clarke (October 2012 General Conference)

How do I keep my covenant to always remember the Savior?

Look up this lesson on the Come Follow Me website. Read the first paragraph and answer the following questions:

What does it mean to always remember the Savior?

....

What do these scriptures teach you about always remembering the Savior?

JOHN 14:26

3 NEPHI 11:32

JOHN 8:29

ALMA 37:36-37

D&C 6:36

D&C 20:77,79

WHAT ARE SOME REASONS PEOPLE FORGET THE LORD? (USE HELAMAN 12:1-5 FOR SOME IDEAS)

Sunday School Curriculum

What do you learn from these three talks that will help you to always remember the Savior?

❖ "O, Remember, Remember" by President Henry B. Eyring (October 2007 General Conference)
❖ "This Do in Remembrance of Me" by Elder Jeffrey R. Holland (October 1995 General Conference)
❖ "To Always Remember Him" by Elder D. Todd Christofferson (*Ensign*, April 2011, 21-27)

How can I prepare to receive temple ordinances?

Ideas What are some specific things that someone can do to prepare to receive temple ordinances? Brainstorm as many ideas as you can think of and continue to fill this box as you study this topic.

Why do you think a temple was chosen for the cover of the current *For the Strength of Youth* pamphlet? For some insight, read the "Message to the Youth from the First Presidency".

_____

_____

_____

_____

_____

_____

_____

_____

PSALM 24:3-4 & D&C 97:15-17 Why do you think spiritual cleanliness is a requirement for entering the temple?

What do you learn from these talks and articles about preparing for temple ordinances?

- ❖ "Prepared in a Manner That Never Had Been Known," by Sister Linda K. Burton (October 2014 General Conference)
- ❖ "Prepare for the Blessings of the Temple" by Elder Russell M. Nelson (*Ensign*, October 2010, 40-51)
- ❖ "Making the Temple a Part of Your Life" (*Ensign*, October 2010, 76-78)
- ❖ "Commonly Asked Questions" (*Ensign*, October 2010, 79-80)

Why is family important?

Study "The Family: A Proclamation to the World" and "Family" in *For the Strength of Youth*. Look for how the family fits into each of these parts of the Plan of Salvation. Record what you find.

Premortal Life	Mortal Life	Postmortal Life

What do these scriptures teach you about the importance of the family?

ROMANS 8:16-17	HEBREWS 12:9	GENESIS 2:18
GENESIS 2:23-24	D&C 131:1-4	D&C 138:48
MOSIAH 4:14-15	D&C 93:40	D&C 93:43
D&C 93:48-50	D&C 68:25	D&C 68:27-29

Young Men/Young Women Curriculum

What do you learn from these talks and articles about why family is important?

- ❖ "Becoming Goodly Parents" by Elder L. Tom Perry (October 2012 General Conference)
- ❖ "The Family Is of God," by Sister Carole M. Stephens (April 2015 General Conference)
- ❖ "Why Marriage, Why Family," Elder D. Todd Christofferson (April 2015 General Conference)

Why is temple marriage important?

Look up this lesson on the Come Follow Me website. Read the first paragraph and answer the following questions:

What is the only way to gain exaltation?

What is exaltation? (see "Eternal Life" in *True to the Faith*)

What assurance does a couple receive when they are sealed in the temple?

What do these scriptures teach you about the importance of temple marriage? Write what you learn from each scripture, words you looked up; and, if there is room, you could include short quotes.

D&C 49:16-17

D&C 131:1-4

D&C 132:15-17

D&C 132:18

D&C 132:19

D&C 132:20-21

Marriage

Look up "Marriage, The New and Everlasting Covenant of Marriage" in *True to the Faith* and write down any important doctrines and principles that are important to understand.

What do you learn from these talks and articles about why temple marriage is important?

- ❖ "Families under Covenant" by President Henry B. Eyring (April 2012 General Conference)
- ❖ "Why Marriage and Family Matter---Everywhere in the World," by Elder L. Tom Perry (April 2015 General Conference)
- ❖ "The Eternal Blessings of Marriage" by Elder Richard G. Scott (April 2011 General Conference)
- ❖ "Our Temple Marriage is Worth any Price" (Liahona, October 2010, 69-70)
- ❖ "The Family: A Proclamation to the World"

Why is chastity important?

WHAT IS CHASTITY IMPORTANT TO THE LORD? Look up the following scriptures and references on this page and write down significant principles and doctrines about chastity.

"CHASTITY", *TRUE TO THE FAITH*

"SEXUAL PURITY" AND "DRESS AND APPEARANCE", *FOR THE STRENGTH OF YOUTH*

1 NEPHI 10:21

ALMA 39:1-13

MORONI 9:9

D&C 46:33

D&C 121:45-46

Joseph of Egypt

What can you learn from Joseph of Egypt about the importance of remaining sexually pure at all costs? In the center column record words you looked up and in the right column write what you are learning.

Reference	Definitions	What I learned
Genesis 39:7-8		
Genesis 39:9		
Genesis 39:10-11		
Genesis 39:12		
Genesis 39:13-15		
Genesis 39:16-20		
Genesis 39:21		

What do you learn from these talks and articles about the importance of chastity?

- ❖ "We Believe in Being Chaste" by Elder David A. Bednar (April 2013 General Conference)
- ❖ "Personal Purity" by Elder Jeffrey R. Holland (*Ensign*, November 1998, 75-78)
- ❖ "Helping Those Who Struggle with Same-Gender Attraction" by Elder Jeffrey R. Holland (Ensign, October 2007, 42-45)
- ❖ "The Plan of Happiness," by Sister Elder Boyd K. Packer (April 2015 General Conference)

_____

_____

_____

_____

_____

_____

_____

_____

_____

What are the Church's standards regarding dating?

13th Article of Faith — Select words or phrases from the 13th Article of Faith and write your thoughts about how they apply to the standards of dating.

DATING

What are the Church's standards for dating? (Look up "Dating" in *For the Strength of Youth*)

Standard of Liberty

Study Alma 46:11-14. How can youth today be like Moroni and raise their own standard of liberties? How can that impact their dating experiences as well as their influence on others?

_____
_____
_____
_____
_____
_____
_____
_____

What do these scriptures have to do with dating?

DEUTERONOMY 7:3-4

D&C 46:33

What do you learn from these talks and articles about the standards of dating?

❖ "Preparation Brings Blessings" by President Thomas S. Monson (April 2010 General Conference)
❖ "Guardians of Virtue" by Sister Elaine S. Dalton (April 2011 General Conference)

_____
_____
_____
_____
_____
_____
_____
_____
_____
_____
_____
_____

How can I prepare now to become a righteous wife and mother?

Look up this lesson on the Come Follow Me website. Read the first paragraph and answer the following question:

What can a young woman do to prepare now to become a righteous wife and mother?

Characteristics of a Righteous Woman

What characteristics of a righteous woman can you find in these scriptures?

Proverbs 31: 10-31

Alma 56:47-48

Moroni 7:45-46

D&C 88:123-125

Preparation

Brainstorm as many ideas as you can of specific things a young woman can do to prepare to become a righteous wife and mother. (Look up D&C 88:78-80, 118; D&C 90:15 and "Education" in *For the Strength of Youth* for ideas)

What do you learn from these talks about preparing to be a righteous wife and mother?

- ❖ "Marriage: Watch and Learn" by Elder L. Whitney Clayton (April 2013 General Conference)
- ❖ "Mothers and Daughters" by Elder M. Russell Ballard (April 2010 General Conference)
- ❖ "Filling Our Homes with Light and Truth" by Sister Cheryl A. Esplin (April 2015 General Conference)
- ❖ "Education," *For the Strength of Youth*

How can I prepare now to become a righteous husband and father?

Look up this lesson on the Come Follow Me website. Read the first paragraph and answer the following question:

What can a young man do to prepare now to become a righteous husband and father?

....

Responsibilities Read *The Family: A Proclamation to the World* and find all of the duties and responsibilities that a young man will have as a husband and father. Record what you find below.

....

What can you learn about being a righteous man and father from these examples?

1 Nephi 2:1-3

1 Nephi 16:14-32

Preparation Brainstorm as many ideas as you can, of specific things that a young man can do to prepare to become a righteous husband and father. (Look up "Work and Self-Reliance" and "Education" in *For the Strength of Youth*, D&C 42:22; 58:26-28; and 107:99-100 for ideas.)

AUGUST: MARRIAGE AND FAMILY

What do you learn from these talks about preparing to be a righteous husband and father?

- ❖ "Marriage: Watch and Learn" by Elder L. Whitney Clayton (April 2013 General Conference)
- ❖ "Fatherhood---Our Eternal Destiny," by Larry M. Gibson (April 2015 General Conference)
- ❖ "Becoming Provident Providers Temporally and Spiritually" by Elder Robert D. Hales (April 2009 General Conference)
- ❖ "Brethren, We Have Work to Do" by Elder D. Todd Christofferson (October 2012 General Conference)

How do the roles of men and women complement each other in families?

Divine Roles

Study *The Family: A Proclamation to the World* and find what it teaches about gender and divine roles of men and women?

Fathers & Husbands	Mothers & Wives

What do these scriptures teach you about the responsibilities of parents?

Proverbs 22:6

D&C 68:25

D&C 121:41-43

Moses 5:1

Alma 53:21

Alma 56:47-48

D&C 25

This section was given to Emma Smith and is counsel to her on how she can support her husband and fulfill her responsibilities. What principles can you find in this section that applies to husbands and wives?

What do you learn from these talks about the complementary roles of men and women?

- ❖ "We'll Ascend Together," by Sister Linda K. Burton (April 2015 General Conference)
- ❖ "Finding Lasting Peace & Building Eternal Families," by Elder L. Tom Perry (October 2015 General Conference)
- ❖ "The Moral Force of Women," by Elder D. Todd Christofferson (October 2013 General Conference)

How can I strengthen my family?

What are some spiritual dangers that are currently threatening the family?

Search "The Family: A Proclamation to the World" and find any principle you can that leads to happiness in family life. Record what you find here.

Lehi's family Study 1 Nephi 16:14-32 and look for ways that Lehi and his family applied the principles you wrote above. Record your thoughts here:

Read "Family" in *For the Strength of Youth* and find things that can strengthen your family. Include any specific ideas you can do to implement those ideas into your home.

What do you learn from these resources about strengthening your family?

- ❖ "More Diligent and Concerned at Home" by Elder David A. Bednar (October 2009 General Conference)
- ❖ "Defenders of the Family Proclamation," by Sister Bonnie L. Oscarson (April 2015 General Conference)
- ❖ 1 Nephi 8:12; D&C 88:119

How will keeping a journal bless me and my family?

Look up this lesson on the Come Follow Me website. Read the first paragraph and answer the following question:

What are some blessings of keeping a journal?

What are some blessings that have come because people in the scriptures kept a record?

1 Nephi 1:1-3

Alma 37:8-9

Moses 6:5

Moses 6:45-46

What types of things did Nephi keep in his record?

1 Nephi 6:3-6

What types of things should we include in our own personal records?

How might this scripture apply to our own efforts in keeping a personal journal?

3 Nephi 23:6-13

What quotes and counsel towards keeping a personal journal can you find in these talks?

- ❖ "The Angels May Quote From It" by President Spencer W. Kimball (*New Era*, February 2003, 32-35)
- ❖ "O Remember, Remember" by President Henry B. Eyring (October 2007 General Conference)

Why is it important to learn about my family history?

Family History Work and Genealogy

What doctrines and principles do you learn from "Family History Work and Genealogy" in *True to the Faith*, that help you understand the importance of learning about your family history?

What doctrines and principles about family history do these scriptures teach you?

1 Corinthians 15:29

1 Peter 3:18-20

1 Peter 4:6

Malachi 4:5-6

D&C 2:1-3

D&C 110:13-16

D&C 128:16-18

What do you learn about the importance of family history from these talks and articles? In the gray box, write specific things we can do to be involved with family history work.

- ❖ "The Joy of Redeeming the Dead" by Elder Richard G. Scott (October 2012 General Conference)
- ❖ "The Hearts of the Children Shall Turn" by Elder David A. Bednar (October 2011 General Conference)
- ❖ "The Book," by Allan F. Packer (October 2014 General Conference)
- ❖ Website: Youth and Family History

-------- Specific Ideas --------

How can I teach others how to do family history work?

Look up this lesson on the Come Follow Me website. Read the first paragraph and answer the following questions:

What things has the Lord given us to perform ordinances for our ancestors?

How can we help others learn about family history?

What important doctrines and principles are taught in these verses that are important for others to understand in order to catch the spirit of family history work?

D&C 128:16-18	D&C 138:46-48

What do you learn about the importance of family history from these talks and articles? Look for things you could share with others who are learning about family history work.

- ❖ "Generations Linked in Love" by Elder Russell M. Nelson (April 2010 General Conference)
- ❖ "The Hearts of the Children Shall Turn" by Elder David A. Bednar (October 2011 General Conference)

How can I explain the importance of marriage and family to others?

Look up this lesson on the Come Follow Me website. What insights do you gain from the opening paragraph?

On this and the next page are 3 questions that someone may ask you. Study the following references and write down everything that you find that helps you answer these questions.

- ❖ "The Family: A Proclamation to the World"
- ❖ "Spiritual Whirlwinds" by Elder Neil L. Andersen (April 2014 General Conference)
- ❖ "Family" in *For the Strength of Youth*
- ❖ "Marriage", True to the Faith
- ❖ "Eternal Marriage", Preach My Gospel, 85-86
- ❖ "Temple Marriage"(MormonNewsroom.org article)
- ❖ "Why Marriage, Why Family" by D. Todd Christofferson (April 2015 General Conference)

Why should I get married and have children?

WHY SHOULD MARRIAGE BE BETWEEN A MAN AND A WOMAN?

HOW CAN I HAVE A STRONG AND HAPPY FAMILY?

What opportunities are there for learning and teaching in the home?

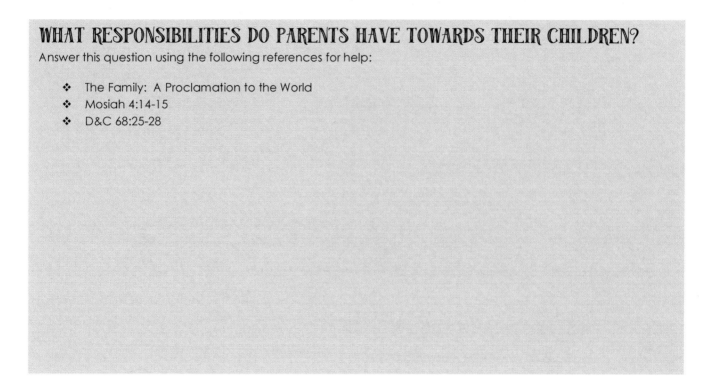

WHAT RESPONSIBILITIES DO PARENTS HAVE TOWARDS THEIR CHILDREN?

Answer this question using the following references for help:

- ❖ The Family: A Proclamation to the World
- ❖ Mosiah 4:14-15
- ❖ D&C 68:25-28

What can you learn from each of these articles and references that could help you to better learn and teach in your current and future home?

"THE LORD IS MY LIGHT" BY ELDER QUENTIN L. COOK (APRIL 2015 GENERAL CONFERENCE)

"FAMILY HOME EVENING" *TRUE TO THE FAITH (65-66)*

"FAMILY PRAYER" *TRUE TO THE FAITH (122)*

"IMPORTANCE OF DAILY SCRIPTURE STUDY" *TRUE TO THE FAITH (155-156)*

How can I be in the world but not of the world?

Look up this lesson on the Come Follow Me website. Read the opening paragraph and write the quote by President Thomas S. Monson here along with your personal thoughts about it.

What does the phrase "to be in the world but not of the world" mean to you?

_____

_____

_____

_____

What do these scriptures teach you about being in the world but not of the world?

2 Kings 6:14-17

Matthew 5:14-16

John 15:19

1 Nephi 8:24-28

1 Nephi 15:23-25

Alma 34:39

Helaman 5:12

D&C 10:5

D&C 27:15-18

D&C 87:8

What can you learn from these talks about being in the world but not of the world?

- ❖ "Yes, We Can and Will Win!"" by Ulisses Soares (April 2015 General Conference)
- ❖ "Which Way Do You Face?" by Lynn G. Robbins (October 2014 General Conference)
- ❖ "Sharing Your Light" by Neill F. Marriott (October 2014 General Conference)

How do I guard my virtue?

Look up this lesson on the Come Follow Me website. Read the opening paragraph and answer the following questions:

What is virtue?

How can we guard our virtue?

What principles and doctrines do these scriptures teach you about remaining virtuous?

Romans 12:21

Genesis 39:1-12

2 Timothy 2:22

Moroni 10:30

D&C 27:15-18

D&C 121:45-46

Isaiah 1:18

Helaman 12:23

D&C 58:42-43

Matthew 5:27-28

Romans 6:12

Alma 39:3-9

D&C 42:23

1 Nephi 17:3

Mosiah 24:14

Alma 26:12

What do you learn about the importance of virtue and guarding it in these places?

"SEXUAL PURITY" *FOR THE STRENGTH OF THE YOUTH, 35-37*

"CHASTITY" *TRUE TO THE FAITH, 29-33*

"PORNOGRAPHY" *TRUE TO THE FAITH, 117-118*

What can you learn from these talks about the importance of guarding our virtue?

- ❖ "Guardians of Virtue" by Sister Elaine S. Dalton (*Ensign*, May 2011, 121-124)
- ❖ "Place No More for the Enemy of My Soul" by Elder Jeffrey R. Holland (April 2010 General Conference)
- ❖ "Can Ye Feel So Now?" by Elder Quentin L. Cook (October 2012 General Conference)
- ❖ "Be of a Good Courage" by Sister Ann M. Dibb (*Ensign*, May 2010, 114-116)
- ❖ "Protection from Pornography" by Sister Linda S. Reeves (April 2014 General Conference)

How do the things I say affect me and those around me?

Study Ephesians 4:29-32. How do the doctrines and principles in these verses apply to the following times words are used in our daily lives?

WORDS WE SAY:

WORDS WE READ:

WORDS WE WRITE/TYPE:

WORDS WE SPEAK:

James 3:2-10 In these verses James uses five analogies as he teaches about the power of our words. Write what you learn about each analogy along with any additional thoughts and insights.

A HORSE BIT

A SHIP

A FOREST FIRE

POISON

A PURE FOUNTAIN

What do these scriptures teach you about the significance and power of words and how we communicate with others?

Proverbs 15:1-4

Proverbs 16:24

1 Timothy 4:12

Alma 31:5

D&C 25:12

D&C 108:7

Exodus 20:7

Matthew 12 :34-37

Matthew 15 :11

Luke 12 :2-3

1 Timothy 5 :13

D&C 42 :27

2 Nephi 32:2-3

D&C 63:61-64

Mosiah 4:30

Language

Study "Language" in *For the Strength of Youth*. Record anything you learn that helps you answer the question, "How do the things I say affect me and those around me?"

Profanity

Study "Profanity" in *True to the Faith*. Record anything you learn that helps you answer the question, "How do the things I say affect me and those around me?"

What can you learn from these talks about the words that we use?

- ❖ "Thy Speech Reveals Thee" by Elder L. Tom Perry (*Liahona*, July 2007, 30-33)
- ❖ "The Tongue of Angels" by Elder Jeffrey R. Holland (April 2007 General Conference)
- ❖ "Arise and Shine Forth" by Sister Ann M. Dibb (*Ensign*, May 2012, 117-119)
- ❖ "What Are You Thinking" by W. Elder Craig Zwick, April 2014 General Conference

Why do we fast?

Fasting and Fast Offerings

What important doctrines and principles can you find in *True to the Faith* ("Fasting and Fast Offerings) that help you understand why we fast?

What specific principles can you find in these scriptures that give insight into fasting?

ESTHER 4:10-17	MATTHEW 4:1-11
ALMA 17:1-3, 9	D&C 59:12-14
ISAIAH 58:3-12	MATTHEW 6:16-18
MOSIAH 27:18-24	ALMA 6:6
ALMA 5:45-46	HELAMAN 3:35

What can you learn from these talks about why we fast? (Make note of good stories you can use when teaching about fasting)

❖ "What Seek Ye?" By Elder L. Tom Perry (April 2005 General Conference)
❖ "Is Not This the Fast That I Have Chosen?" by President Henry B. Eyring (April 2015 General Conference)

Why are we commanded to keep the Sabbath day holy?

Look up this lesson on the Come Follow Me website. Read the opening paragraph and answer the following questions:

Who is the Sabbath day for?

What does observing the Sabbath show?

What blessings do we receive when we keep the Sabbath day holy?

Sabbath

What important doctrines and principles can you find in *True to the Faith* (under "Sabbath") that help you understand the importance of the Sabbath and how to keep it holy?

Sabbath Day Observance

What important doctrines and principles can you find in *For the Strength of Youth* (under "Sabbath Day Observance") that help you understand the importance of the Sabbath and how to keep it holy?

What can you learn from these talks about why we keep the Sabbath day Holy? In the gray box include specific ideas of things we can do on the Sabbath day. (Make note of good stories you can use when teaching about the Sabbath)

- ❖ "Continually Holding Fast" by Elder Kevin S. Hamilton (October 2013 General Conference)
- ❖ "The Sabbath Is a Delight" by President Russell M. Nelson (April 2015 General Conference)
- ❖ "Anchors of Testimony" by Sister Mary N. Cook (April 2008 General Conference)

What do these scriptures teach you about the Sabbath Day?

Genesis 2:2

Exodus 20:8-11

Exodus 31:13

Isaiah 58:13-14

Luke 23:55-24:1

D&C 59:9-13

Mosiah 13:16-19

Why is it important to be honest?

What are some reasons you think that people choose to be dishonest?

What are consequences (positive and negative) of being dishonest? (It is generally for the positive consequences that people choose to be dishonest – however there are also negative consequences attached to that choice.)

What are consequences (positive and negative) of being honest?

Honesty and Integrity What important doctrines and principles can you find in *For the Strength of Youth* (under "Honesty and Integrity") that help you understand the importance of being honest? (Pay special attention to the consequences.)

Honesty What important doctrines and principles can you find in *True to the Faith* (under "Honesty") that help you understand the importance of being honest? (Pay special attention to the consequences.)

What can you learn from these talks about the importance of being honest?

- ❖ "Preparation Brings Blessings" by President Thomas S. Monson (April 2010 General Conference)
- ❖ "What Shall a Man Give in Exchange for His Soul" by Elder Robert C. Gay (October 2012 General Conference)
- ❖ "I Believe in Being Honest and True" by Sister Ann Dibb (April 2011 General Conference)

_____
_____
_____
_____
_____
_____
_____
_____
_____
_____
_____
_____

What can you find in these scriptures that teach about the importance of honesty and inspiration to be honest in our own lives?

Psalm 101:7
_____

Proverbs 12:22
_____

2 Corinthians 4:2
_____

Ephesians 4:29
_____

Alma 27:27
_____

Article of Faith #13
_____

Acts 5:1-10
_____

2 Nephi 9:34
_____

Alma 12:1-5
_____

Joseph Smith-History 1:21-25

Why do we pay tithing?

How has your testimony of tithing grown throughout your life?

_____
_____
_____
_____
_____
_____
_____

What are some of the promises made to those who pay their tithing?

MALACHI 3:8-10	3 NEPHI 24:8-10	D&C 64:23

What does D&C 119 teach about what the Lord expects us to pay in tithes? (Tip: "interest" refers to annual income)

What does "Tithes and Offerings" in *For the Strength of Youth* teach you about the following principles? Write what you find in the appropriate column.

BLESSINGS	HOW FUNDS ARE USED	ATTITUDE

What can you learn from these talks about the importance of paying tithing?

❖ "The Blessings of Tithing" by President Henry B. Eyring (*Liahona*, June 2011, 4-5)
❖ "The Windows of Heaven" by Elder David A. Bednar (October 2013 General Conference)
❖ "Like a Watered Garden" by Elder Jeffrey R. Holland (October 2001 General Conference)
❖ "We Walk By Faith) by President Gordon B. Hinckley (April 2002 General Conference)
❖ "Tithing," *True to the Faith*

How do the commandments help me learn to be more like Heavenly Father?

Look up this lesson on the Come Follow Me website. Read the opening paragraph and list the important principles you would want others to understand about the purpose of commandments.

How has your attitude and understanding of commandments changed as you have grown older?

_____

_____

_____

_____

_____

_____

Below are scriptures about commandments. Study each one and note the principles you learn about the commandments and the purpose of them.

DEUTERONOMY 10:12-13

D&C 82:8-10

MATTHEW 22:34-40

JOHN 14:15

1 JOHN 5:1-3

D&C 88:22

D&C 93:20

What can you learn from these talks and articles about the importance of keeping the commandments?

- ❖ "Forget Me Not" by President Dieter F. Uchtdorf (October 2011 General Conference)
- ❖ "If Thou Wilt Enter into Life, Keep the Commandments" by Elder Robert D. Hales (April 1996 General Conference)
- ❖ "As Many As I Love, I Rebuke and Chasten" by Elder D. Todd Christofferson (April 2011 General Conference)
- ❖ "Obedience," *True to the Faith*

How can I help others understand my standards?

What are some words or phrases in these scriptures that indicate what our attitude should be when talking about our standards with others?

ROMANS 1:16

2 TIMOTHY 1:7-8

2 NEPHI 8:7

1 TIMOTHY 4:12

3 NEPHI 11:29

D&C 11:21

D&C 84:85

D&C 100:5-8

Obedience Look up "Obedience" in True to the Faith and look for information in this paragraph that would help you respond to someone who thinks that commandments are too restrictive.

Preparation Brings Blessings Read the talk "Preparation Brings Blessings" by President Thomas S. Monson (April 2010 General Conference). Look at how he explains certain standards and what you can learn from how he does it.

How does keeping the commandments affect my ability to learn the Gospel?

Study these three examples in the scriptures of individuals who were blessed with knowledge and understanding because of their obedience. Record what you learn from each story as well as how we may find ourselves in similar situations for each example.

Daniel, Shadrach, Meshach and Abed-Nego
Daniel 1

Nephi
1 Nephi 4

Joseph Smith
Joseph-Smith History 1:11-17

What do these scriptures teach you about the relationship of keeping the commandments and gospel learning?

John 7:17

2 Nephi 28:30

D&C 42:61

D&C 50:24

D&C 76:5-10

What specific counsel can you find in these talks?

❖ "Obedience Brings Blessings" by President Thomas S. Monson (April 2013 General Conference)
❖ "A Living Testimony" by President Henry B. Eyring (April 2011 General Conference)
❖ "How to Obtain Revelation and Inspiration for Your Personal Life" by Elder Richard G. Scott April 2012 General Conference)

How can I inspire others to obey the commandments?

Example What do these scriptures teach you about the importance of being an example?

Matthew 5:14-16

1 Timothy 4:12

Alma 17:11

Alma 39:11

What does **Alma 4:19** teach you about how to inspire others?

The following scriptures are examples of people living the principles you wrote about above. Study them and record what is inspiring to you about them.

Matthew 16:13-19

Mosiah 3:17

Alma 5:45-48

Alma 7:13

D&C 76:22-24

What can you learn about being an example and inspiring others from these talks and article?

❖ "Perfect Love Casteth Out Fear" by Elder L. Tom Perry (October 2011 General Conference)
❖ "Arise and Shine Forth" by Sister Ann M. Dibb (April 2012 General Conference)
❖ "Living What You Teach" *Teaching No Greater Call*, page 18-19

What blessings does Heavenly Father promise if I obey the commandments?

Look up this lesson on the Come Follow Me website. Read the opening paragraph and list the important principles you feel are important to understand about the blessings that come from keeping the Commandments.

What promises are given to the youth if they keep the commandments in the "Message to the Youth from the First Presidency" at the beginning of *For the Strength of Youth*?

What warnings do these scriptures give for not keeping the commandments?

Jeremiah 7:23-24

D&C 1:14-15

D&C 58:29-33

What do these scriptures teach you about the blessings God has for us when we keep the Commandments?

D&C 130:20-21

D&C 82:10

Look up these scriptures and find where the Lord promises certain blessings for those who keep His commandments. Record what you find below.

Commandments	Blessings
Isaiah 58:6-11	
Malachi 3:10-12	
D&C 14:7	
D&C 20:77,79	
D&C 59:9-20	
D&C 89:18-21	

Obedience

What do you learn about receiving promised blessings from "Obedience" in *True to the Faith*?

Promise People Blessings

What insight and guidelines can you find in "Promise People Blessings" in *Preach My Gospel*?

_____

_____

_____

_____

_____

_____

_____

_____

_____

_____

_____

_____

_____

_____

How can I become more Christlike?

Look up this lesson on the Come Follow Me website. Read the opening paragraph and list the important principles you would want others to understand about becoming more Christlike.

Study the following Christlike attributes listed in "How Do I Develop Christlike Attributes" in *Preach My Gospel*. In the center column write everything you learn about that attribute and in the right, record specific things you can do to grow in that area in your life.

	About the Attribute	What I can do
Faith		
Hope		
Charity and Love		
Virtue		
Knowledge		
Patience		
Humility		
Diligence		
Obedience		

Christ's Attributes

What attributes of Christ can you see in these verses and reference?

Matthew 26:36-45

Matthew 26:50-52

Luke 23:33-34

John 19:25-27

3 Nephi 17

The Living Christ

What do these scriptures teach you about YOURSELF and the attributes you wrote above?

3 Nephi 12:48

Moroni 7:48

Mosiah 3:19

What can you learn about becoming more Christlike in these talks?

- ❖ "Ponder the Path of Thy Feet" by President Thomas S. Monson, October 2014 General Conference
- ❖ "The Challenge to Become" by Elder Dallin H. Oaks (October 2000 General Conference)
- ❖ "Yes, Lord, I Will Follow Thee" by Elder Eduardo Gavarett, October 2014 General Conference

How can I develop Christlike love?

Look up this lesson on the Come Follow Me website. Read the opening paragraph and list the important principles you would want others to understand about what Christlike love is and how we develop it.

What doctrines and principles do you learn about Christlike love from these scriptures?

Moroni 7:45-48

3 Nephi 12:44

Mosiah 4:16

1 John 4:7-11

1 John 4:18-21

John 15:9-13

1 Samuel 16:7

Leviticus 19:18

Examples of those with Christlike love

Luke 23:33-34

Alma 61:9

Genesis 45

Charity

What important principles do you learn from "charity" in *True to the Faith*?

What can you learn about developing Christlike love in these talks?

- ❖ "Love- the Essence of the Gospel" by President Thomas S. Monson (April 2014 General Conference)
- ❖ "The Merciful Obtain Mercy" by President Dieter F. Uchtdorf (April 2012 General Conference)
- ❖ "Loving Others and Living with Differences" by Elder Dallin H. Oaks (October 2014 General Conference)

_____

_____

_____

_____

_____

_____

_____

_____

_____

_____

_____

_____

_____

_____

_____

_____

_____

_____

How can I be more Christlike in my service to others?

What important principle does **John 13:34-35** teach about what Christlike service is?

_____

_____

_____

_____

_____

_____

Examples of Christ giving service

Summarize what Christ did in each of these scriptures to serve others.

Matthew 14:13-21

John 9:1-7

John 13:4-5, 12-17

1 Nephi 11:31

3 Nephi 17:5-9

What important principles do these scriptures teach about Christlike service?

Mosiah 2:17

Matthew 20:27

Matthew 25:31-46

John 13:34-35

The Parable of the Good Samaritan

Study Luke 10:25-37 and answer the following questions as you study.

What did the lawyer ask Jesus?

How did Christ answer him?

What did the lawyer then ask Jesus?

What did Jesus answer in return?

What, then, did the lawyer say? (Tip: The lawyer was trying to trap Jesus; he wasn't really asking sincerely.)

Where was the "certain man" going?

What happened to him?

Tip: The temple priests and Levites often lived in Jericho, so this could very well have been an individual returning from serving in the temple. Also, it was not uncommon for thieves to hide out and attack travelers who were alone.

What did the "certain priest" do?

Tip: This would have been a priest from Jericho likely either going or returning from serving in the temple.

Why should this Priest have stopped and helped?

What did the Levite do?

Tip: Levites also worked in the temple and assisted the Priests.

Why should the Levite have stopped to help?

What could have been some of the reasons the Priest and Levite didn't stop?

What did the Samaritan do?

Tip: Samaritans came from Samaria and the population was a mix of both Gentiles and Jews. They were bitter rivals of the Jews.

What are all of the lessons you can learn from this parable?

OCTOBER: BECOMING MORE CHRISTLIKE

What can you learn about being more Christlike in your service from these talks and articles?

- ❖ "We Never Walk Alone" by President Thomas S. Monson (October 2013 General Conference)
- ❖ "You Are My Hands" by President Dieter F. Uchtdorf (April 2010 General Conference)
- ❖ "First Observe, Then Serve" by Sister Linda K. Burton (October 2012 General Conference)
- ❖ "Service," *For the Strength of Youth*
- ❖ "Truly Good and Without Guile" by Elder Michael T. Ringwood (April 2015 General Conference)

How can I learn to be more patient?

Look up this lesson on the Come Follow Me website. Read the opening paragraph and list the important principles about patience and how to develop it.

Look up the following scriptures and write in the correct column what principles you learn about patience and impatience.

Patience	*Impatience*
Psalm 37:7-9	
Hebrews 10:35-36	
Mosiah 23:21-22	
Alma 26:27	
D&C 24:8	
Romans 5:3	
James 1:3-4	
Mosiah 3:19	

JOB "The patience of Job" is a common phrase that people use to refer to someone who has an incredible amount of patience. Review his life by reading about him in the Bible Dictionary, reviewing the chapter headings in the Book of Job, and reading Job 1 and 19:25-26. Record what you learn from him here.

OCTOBER: BECOMING MORE CHRISTLIKE

What can you learn about developing patience from these talks?

- ❖ "Continue in Patience" by President Dieter F. Uchtdorf (April 2010 General Conference)
- ❖ "Waiting upon the Lord: Thy Will Be Done" by Elder Robert D. Hales (October 2011 General Conference)
- ❖ "The Power of Patience" by Elder Robert C. Oaks (October 2006 General Conference)

Why is it important to be grateful?

The Ten Lepers

Study **Luke 17:11-19** and answer the following questions as you study.

Verses 11- 12: What was a "leper"? (For help, look up "Leper" and "Leprosy" in the Bible Dictionary)

Why do you think the lepers were standing "afar off"? What kind of a life would they have been living up to this point?

Verse 13: If you were able to see this moment, how do you imagine they would have said this phrase? What would be the tone and urgency in their voices?

Verse 14: Tip: A leper who had been healed was not allowed to enter back into society unless a priest pronounced them clean. Notice in this verse *when* they were healed. What does this teach you?

Verses 15 - 19: What do you think may have been some of the reasons that the nine lepers didn't return to give thanks?

What did the "one" do to show that he was grateful?

Why did the Lord call him a "stranger"? Tip: Look up "Samaritans" in the Bible Dictionary. What does this suggest to you about the other nine?

What are all of the lessons you can learn from this story?

What do you learn about being grateful from these scriptures?

Psalm 92:1

Psalm 100

Alma 26:8

Alma 37:37

D&C 46:32

D&C 59:15-21

D&C 78:19

Gratitude What important principles do learn from "Gratitude" in *For the Strength of Youth*?

What can you learn about the importance of being grateful from these talks?

❖ "The Divine Gift of Gratitude" by President Thomas S. Monson (October 2010 General Conference)
❖ "Grateful in Any Circumstances" by President Dieter F. Uchtdorf (April 2014 General Conference)
❖ "Thanks Be to God" by Elder Russell M. Nelson (April 2012 General Conference)

How can I invite others to become more like the Savior?

ASK DIRECT QUESTIONS Look up "Ask Direct Questions" in *Preach My Gospel* (page 197). What principles will help you know how to talk to others and help them overcome habits so they can become more like the Savior?

What blessings can you find in these scriptures that are given to those who come unto Christ?

MATTHEW 11:28-30   MORONI 10:32

What can you learn from Christ's example when he invited others to come unto Him and live righteously?

MARK 10:17-22   LUKE 10:25-37

ASK DIRECT QUESTIONS Look up "How Do I Help People Make and Keep Commitments?" in *Preach My Gospel* (pages 195-201). What principles can help you invite others to become more like the Savior?

What can you learn from these talks that can help you invite others to become more like the Savior?

- ❖ "Come Unto Christ" by President Henry B. Eyring (Ensign, March 2008, 49-52)
- ❖ "Let Us Raise Our Voice of Warning" by President Henry B. Eyring (Ensign, January 2009, 2-7)

How can I show love for those I teach?

What does charity look like? Study Moroni 7:45. To the left are different attributes of charity found in that verse. In the center column write what you think each attribute means and looks like in someone living that attribute. In the right column consider what that attribute would look like in a teacher or someone who is sharing the gospel with others.

	What this attribute means	What this attribute would be like in a teacher
Suffereth Long		
Is Kind		
Envieth Not		
Is Not Puffed Up		
Seeketh Not Her Own		
Note Easily Provoked		
Thinketh No Evil		
Rejoiceth Not In Iniquity		
Rejoiceth in Truth		
Beareth All Things		
Believeth All Things		
Hopeth All Things		
Endureth All Things		

What do these scriptures teach you about showing love for those you teach?

John 13:34

Mosiah 28:1-3

Alma 17:21-39

Alma 20:21-27

Moroni 7:46

Love Those You Teach

Study "Love Those You Teach" in *Teaching No Greater Call* (pages 31-39). Record any important principles you learn as you study.

Read "Examples of Great Teachers" by President Thomas S. Monson (*Ensign*, June 2007, 74-80). Record what you learn about loving those you teach.

_____

_____

_____

_____

_____

_____

_____

_____

_____

Sunday School Curriculum

How did the Savior compare gospel truths to familiar objects and experiences?

Look up this lesson on the Come Follow Me website. Read the opening paragraph and list the important principles there that help you understand how the Savior taught.

Parables   Here are some popular parables that Christ used when teaching gospel truths. Read each one and to the left write a summary of the parable and on the right record the gospel truths he taught.

Matthew 20:1-15   LABORERS IN THE VINEYARD

Matthew 25:1-13   TEN VIRGINS

Matthew 25:14-30   TALENTS

Luke 8:4-15   SOWER

Luke 15:1-7   LOST SHEEP

Luke 15:8-10   LOST SILVER

Luke 15:11-32   PRODIGAL (LOST) SON

Objects   Here are some examples of when Christ used objects to teach a gospel truth.   Record what gospel truths he taught and the objects he used to do this.

Matthew 18:1-6

Matthew 5:13-16

Stories   Study "Stories" in *Teaching No Greater Call* (179-182) and write what you learn about why parables and stories are good teaching tools.

Comparisons and Object Lessons

Study "Comparisons and Object Lessons" in *Teaching No Greater Call* (163-164) and write what you learn about teaching using familiar objects.

How do the following brethren use comparisons and familiar objects to teach gospel truths?

Elder L. Tom Perry   "The Doctrines and Principles Contained in the Articles of Faith," *Ensign*, November 2013

Elder Jeffrey R. Holland   "The Laborers in the Vineyard," *Ensign*, May 2012, 31-33

Elder David A. Bednar   "Ye Must Be Born Again," *Ensign*, May 2007, 19-22

How can I use the scriptures to help others become more Christlike?

Look up this lesson on the Come Follow Me website. Read the opening paragraph and list the important principles there that help you understand how to use the scriptures to help others become more Christlike.

Study how the Savior used scriptures to teach others. Look for how those scriptures influenced those he was teaching, and why he used the specific scriptures he did.

MATTHEW 12:1-8	MATTHEW 13:38-41
LUKE 4:17-27	3 NEPHI 23:1-6

What guidelines can you find about teaching from the scriptures in *Preach My Gospel* (pages 180-181)?

What do you learn about the importance of providing context when teaching from the scriptures? (*Teaching, No Greater Call*, pages 54-55)

What can you learn from these talks that can help you use the scriptures to help others become more Christlike?

❖ "Teach From the Scriptures" (In the article "Teaching and Learning in the Church) by Elder Jeffrey R. Holland, *Ensign*, June 2007, 94-97
❖ "Teaching From the Scriptures" in *Teaching No Greater Call*, 54-59

How can I use questions effectively as I teach?

Look up this lesson on the Come Follow Me website. Read the opening paragraph and list the important principles there that help you understand how to use questions effectively as you teach.

Below are four times when either the Savior or Alma used questions to teach people. In the first blank column, record the questions asked. In the second column, record why you think those questions were used. In the right column, write your thoughts about how the teaching experiences might have been different If questions hadn't been used.

	QUESTIONS ASKED	WHY	IF NO QUESTIONS HAD BEEN USED
MATTHEW 7:7-11			
MATTHEW 16:13-17			
MATTHEW 16:24-26			
ALMA 5:14-30			

Teaching With Questions

Study "Teaching with Questions" in *Teaching, No Greater Call* (68-70). Take your notes about the following things on this page.

General Guidelines for Preparing Questions:

General Guidelines for Asking Questions:

Creative Uses of Questions:

What can I learn about gospel learning from the Savior's example?

Look up this lesson on the Come Follow Me website. Read the opening paragraph and list the important principles there that help you understand gospel learning.

What attributes of a good learner can you find in these scriptures? Some of the scriptures are examples of Christ. Pay close attention to how he learned and grew.

Luke 2:40-52

John 5:30

1 Corinthians 2:14

D&C 1:26-28

D&C 112:10

D&C 93:11-20

D&C 130:18-19

What can you learn from these talks that can help you become a better gospel learner?

- ❖ "Acquiring Spiritual Knowledge" by Elder Richard G. Scott (October 1993 General Conference)
- ❖ "Being Teachable" by Elder Robert R. Steuer (April 2002 General Conference)

What does it mean to be self-reliant

Look up this lesson on the Come Follow Me website. Read the opening paragraph and list the important principles there that help you understand what it means to be self-reliant.

What important principles do you learn about self-reliance from these sources?

WORK AND SELF-RELIANCE *For the Strength of Youth, 40-41*

WELFARE: BECOMING SELF-RELIANT *True to the Faith, 184-186*

SELF-RELIANCE *Handbook 2: Administering the Church, 6.1.1*

TEMPORAL SELF-RELIANCE *Daughters in My Kingdom: The History and Work of Relief Society, 51-56*

What do these scriptures teach you about spiritual and/or temporal self-reliance?

2 THESSALONIANS 3:10-13	GALATIANS 6:3-5	D&C 58:26-28	D&C 88:118
D&C 89:18-20	D&C 104:78	MATTHEW 25:1-13	MATTHEW 25:14-29

What can you learn about self-reliance from these talks?

❖ "Meeting the Challenges of Today's World" by Elder Robert D. Hales (October 2015 General Conference)
❖ "Spiritual Preparedness: Start Early and Be Steady" by President Henry B. Eyring (October 2005 General Conference)

_____
_____
_____
_____
_____
_____
_____
_____
_____
_____
_____
_____
_____
_____
_____
_____
_____

How do I know if I am becoming converted?

What do the following people teach you about becoming converted? What was the process of conversion for them and how did conversion impact their lives?

ENOS Enos 1:1-19, 26-27	KING BENJAMIN'S PEOPLE Mosiah 5:1-5
ALMA THE YOUNGER Mosiah 27:23-27	LAMANITES Alma 23:6-7
NEPHITES Helaman 3:35	NEPHITES 4 Nephi 1:1-4,15

Conversion

What important things do you learn about "conversion" in *True to the Faith*?

What do you learn about becoming converted from the following talks?

❖ "Converted unto the Lord" by Elder David A. Bednar (October 2012 General Conference)
❖ "Be Ye Converted" by Sister Bonnie L. Oscarson (October 2013 General Conference)

Why is it important for me to gain an education and develop skills?

Look up the following scriptures and find reasons WHY gaining an education and developing skills is important and HOW to do this. Write what you find in the applicable column.

	Why	How
Proverbs 4:7		
2 Nephi 9:29		
D&C 88:76-80		
D&C 88:118		
D&C 90:15		
D&C 93:36		
D&C 130:18-19		
Proverbs 31:10-31		
Joseph-Smith History 1:11-17		
1 Nephi 11:1-6		
D&C 138:1-11		

Look up "*Education*" and "Work and Self-Reliance" in *For the Strength of Youth*. Record any answers you find for: "Why is it important for me to gain an education and develop skills?"

EDUCATION

WORK AND SELF-RELIANCE

Read Sister Mary N. Cook's talk, "Seek Learning: You Have a Work to Do" (April 2012 General Conference). Record what you learn about the importance of gaining an education and developing skills.

Why is work and important gospel principle?

What principles of work can you find in these scriptures?

GENESIS 3:19	GALATIANS 6:3-5	1 THESSALONIANS 4:11	MOSIAH 10:4-5	PROVERBS 31:27
ALMA 38:12	D&C 58:27	D&C 60:13	D&C 75:29	MOSES 1:39

WORK AND SELF-RELIANCE What do you learn about work being an important gospel principle in "Work and Self-Reliance" in *For the Strength of Youth*?

What can you learn from these talks about work being an important gospel principle?

❖ "Two Principles for Any Economy" by President Dieter F. Uchtdorf (October 2009 General Conference)
❖ "The Blessing of Work" by Bishop H. David Burton (*Ensign*, December 2009, 43-46)

Why does the Lord want me to be healthy?

Look up this lesson on the Come Follow Me website. Read the opening paragraph and list the important principles there that help you understand why the Lord wants us to be healthy.

What counsel can you find in these scriptures that can help you to keep your mind and body healthy?

1 CORINTHIANS 6:19

D&C 88:124

D&C 89:5-9

D&C 89:10-16

D&C 89:18-21

PHYSICAL AND EMOTIONAL HEALTH What do you learn about why the Lord wants us to be healthy in *For the Strength of Youth*?

Study President Boyd K. Packer's talk, "The Word of Wisdom: The Principle and the Promises," (April 1996 General Conference). What does this talk teach you about why the Lord wants us to be healthy?

What is the Lord's way for providing for the poor and needy?

Look up this lesson on the Come Follow Me website. Read the opening paragraph and list the important principles there that help you understand the Lord's way for providing for the poor and needy.

What principles can you find in these scriptures about how the Lord feels about providing for the poor and needy, specific ways he cares for the poor, and warnings for those who do not?

D&C 104:15-18

Isaiah 58:6-11

Malachi 3:8-10

Matthew 25:35-40

D&C 82:18-19

James 1:27

Mosiah 18:27-28

D&C 42:29-30

Alma 34:27-28

Mormon 8:35-37

D&C 56:16-18

D&C 70:14

What can you learn from these talks and articles about the Lord's way for providing for the poor and needy?

- ❖ "Opportunities to Do Good" by President Henry B. Eyring (April 2011 General Conference)
- ❖ "Are We Not All Beggars" by Elder Jeffrey R. Holland (October 2014 General Conference)
- ❖ "God Be With You Till We Meet Again" by President Thomas S. Monson (October 2012 General Conference)
- ❖ "Members' Efforts to Care for the Poor and Needy and Give Service" (Handbook 2: Administering in the Church [2010], 6.1.2)

NOVEMBER: SPIRITUAL AND TEMPORAL SELF-RELIANCE

How can I find solutions to my challenges and problems?

Look up this lesson on the Come Follow Me website. Read the opening paragraph and list the important principles there that help you know how to find solutions to your own challenges and problems.

What principles can you find in these scriptures to help you find solutions to your challenges and problems?

PROVERBS 3:5-6	MATTHEW 11:28-30	MARK 4:36-39
ALMA 7:11-13	ALMA 37:35-37	ALMA 38:5

What can you learn from these talks about finding solutions to your challenges and problems?

- ❖ "We Never Walk Alone" by President Thomas S. Monson (October 2013 General Conference)
- ❖ "Like a Broken Vessel" by Elder Jeffrey R. Holland (October 2013 General Conference)
- ❖ "Make the Exercise of Faith Your First Priority" by Elder Richard G. Scott (October 2014 General Conference)
- ❖ "Physical and Emotional Health," *For the Strength of Youth*

How can I become spiritually self-reliant?

Look up this lesson on the Come Follow Me website. Read the opening paragraph and list the important principles there that help you know how to find solutions to your own challenges and problems.

What do you learn about spiritual self-reliance from these scriptures?

Mormon 9:27

Mormon 10:3-5

D&C 58:26-28

D&C 130:18-19

What do you learn about becoming spiritually self-reliant from these sources?

TESTIMONY *True to the Faith*

THE PARABLE OF THE TEN VIRGINS Matthew 25:1-13

What can you learn from these talks about becoming spiritually self-reliant?

- ❖ "The Power of a Personal Testimony" by President Dieter F. Uchtdorf (October 2006 General Conference)
- ❖ "Approaching the Throne of God with Confidence" by Elder Jorg Klebingat (October 2014 Gen. Conf.)
- ❖ "Converted Unto the Lord" by Elder David A. Bednar (October 2012 General Conference)
- ❖ "Dare to Stand Alone" President Thomas S. Monson (October 2011 General Conference)

How can I find answers to my own gospel questions?

Look up this lesson on the Come Follow Me website. Read the opening paragraph and list the important principles there that help you know how to find solutions to your own challenges and problems.

What do these scriptures teach you about the importance of asking questions?

MATTHEW 7:7	D&C 6:14-15	D&C 9:8-9

Examples of individuals who found answers to their questions
What can you learn from these examples in the scriptures?

Alma 40:1-12

Ether 2:18-23

Joseph-Smith History 1:10-18

Examples of individuals who did not find answers to their questions
What can you learn from these examples in the scriptures?

1 Nephi 15:2-11

What can you learn from these talks and article about finding answers to our questions?

- ❖ "Lord, I Believe" by Elder Jeffrey R. Holland (April 2013 General Conference)
- ❖ "The Reflection in the Water" by President Dieter F. Uchtdorf (CES Fireside for young adults, November 1, 2009)
- ❖ "The Book of Mormon Answers Questions of the Soul," Preach My Gospel (107-108)

How can I overcome doubt with faith?

Look up this lesson on the Come Follow Me website. Read the opening paragraph and list the important principles that stand out to you.

Study this scripture and record important principles you find in these verses.

Mark 9:14-27

Read Elder Jeffrey R. Holland's talk, "Lord, I Believe," (April 2013 General Conference). In the left column record the three observations he made about the story he tells. In the right column record how these observations can assist you in helping someone you know who is experiencing doubt.

1

2

3

How could these scriptures help someone strengthen their faith when dealing with doubt or difficult questions?

1 Nephi 15:24

Helaman 5:12

D&C 6:36

John 7:17

James 2:17-18

2 Nephi 2:11

D&C 46:10-14

Read the analogy about oxygen masks in Elder Neil L. Andersen's talk, "Joseph Smith," (October 2014 General Conference). What does this analogy teach you about strengthening your faith and overcoming doubt?

Read Sister Rosemary M. Wixom's talk, "Returning to Faith," (April 2015 General Conference), and Elder L Whitney Clayton's talk, "Choose to Believe," (April 2015 General Conference). Record what you learn about overcoming doubt with faith.

How can I learn to make my own decisions?

Look up this lesson on the Come Follow Me website. Read the opening paragraph and list the important principles there that help you know how to find solutions to your own challenges and problems.

How can you apply the principles in these verses to decisions you make in your life?

Alma 37:37

D&C 9:7-9

D&C 58:26-29

What can you learn from these talks about learning to make our own decisions?

- ❖ "Good, Better, Best" by Elder Dallin H. Oaks (October 2007 General Conference)
- ❖ "To the Aaronic Priesthood: Preparing for the Decade of Decision" by Elder Robert D. Hales (April 2007 General Conference)
- ❖ "Using the Supernal Gift of Prayer" by Elder Richard G. Scott (April 2007 General Conference)

How can setting goals help me become self-reliant?

Look up this lesson on the Come Follow Me website. Read the opening paragraph and list the important principles there that help you know how to set goals and become self-reliant.

What are some meaningful goals you have set in your life? How did those goals make a difference?

_____

_____

_____

_____

_____

_____

_____

_____

_____

What principles can you find in these verses about the importance of setting goals?

D&C 58:27-29

Alma 34:32-33

2 Nephi 32:9

Philippians 3:13-14

Sometimes we have to prioritize our goals and choose to set some things aside in order to achieve the goals that are the most important to us. What principles do these scriptures teach about this?

1 Kings 18:21

Matthew 6:24

What can you learn from these sources about setting goals and becoming self-reliant?

- ❖ "Choose Wisely" by Elder Quentin L. Cook (October 2014 General Conference)
- ❖ "Raising the Bar" by Elder L. Tom Perry (October 2007 General Conference)
- ❖ "How to Set Goals," *Preach My Gospel*, 146
- ❖ "To the Rescue" by President Thomas S. Monson (April 2001 General Conference)

How can I prepare to be financially self-reliant?

Look up this lesson on the Come Follow Me website. Read the opening paragraph and list the important principles there that help you know how to become financially self-reliant.

Search the following scriptures and look for what the Lord tells us about money. List what you find below.

What the Lord tells us about money

2 Nephi 9:30

2 Nephi 9:51

Jacob 2:13-14

Jacob 2:17-19

Alma 1:29-30

Alma 4:6-8

D&C 19:35

Malachi 3:10-11

What do you learn about being financially self-reliant in the following sources?

Debt *True to the Faith, 48-49*

TITHES AND OFFERINGS *For the Strength of Youth, 38-39*

ALL IS SAFELY GATHERED IN: FAMILY FINANCES *Link to pamphlet found in this lesson on the Come Follow Me Website.*

BECOMING PROVIDENT PROVIDERS TEMPORALLY AND SPIRITUALLY Elder Robert D. Hales, April 2009 General Conference

How can I stand as a witness of God?

What do these nine scriptures teach you about standing as a witness of God?

1 Nephi 8:24-34

Romans 1:16-17

1 Timothy 4:12

1 Peter 3:12-17

D&C 100:5-8

1 Nephi 17:48-55

Mosiah 13:1-9

Mosiah 17:1-4

Moroni 1:1-3

What important things does this talk teach you about standing as a witness of God? "Be Strong and of Good Courage" by President Thomas S. Monson (April 2014 General Conference)

What important things does this talk teach you about standing as a witness of God? "The Cost - and Blessings – of Discipleship" by Elder Jeffrey R. Holland (April 2014 General Conference)

What important things does this talk teach you about standing as a witness of God? "Spiritual Whirlwinds" by Elder Neil L. Andersen, April 2014 General Conference)

How Can I Invite Others to Come Unto Christ?

What do these scriptures teach you about inviting others to come unto Christ?

1 Timothy 4:12	1 Peter 3:15	Mosiah 18:9
D&C 28:16	D&C 100:3-8	D&C 84:85

What important teachings can you find in chapter 5 ("Missionary Work") in *Preach My Gospel* that helps you know how you can invite others to come unto Christ?

_____

_____

_____

_____

_____

_____

_____

_____

_____

_____

_____

_____

_____

_____

_____

_____

_____

_____

_____

_____

What can you learn from these sources about inviting others to come unto Christ? Make note of special quotes and stories you could use as you are teaching.

- ❖ "Put Your Trust in the Lord" by Elder M. Russell Ballard (October 2013 General Conference)
- ❖ "I Have Given You an Example" by Elder Richard G. Scott (April 2014 General Conference)
- ❖ "Come and See" by Elder David A. Bednar (October 2014 General Conference)

How does Heavenly Father want me to use my spiritual gifts?

Look up this lesson on the Come Follow Me website. Read the opening paragraph and list the important principles there that help you understand what spiritual gifts are and how to use them.

Write everything you learn about Spiritual gifts (from the following sources and any other you find) in the appropriate boxes. Include the references next to each note.

What are spiritual gifts?

How does Heavenly Father want me to use my gifts?

How do I identify my spiritual gifts?

Who is given spiritual gifts?

What are some examples of spiritual gifts?

Spiritual Gifts

"Spiritual Gifts," True to the Faith
Article of Faith #7
D&C 46:11-12
1 Corinthians 12:3-27
Moroni 10:8-18

What can you learn from these sources about using your spiritual gifts like Heavenly Father wants you to? Make note of special quotes and stories you could use as you are teaching.

- ❖ "Help Them Aim High" by President Henry B. Eyring (October 2012 General Conference)
- ❖ "Quick to Observe" by Elder David A. Bednar (Ensign, December 2006, 31-36)

How can I prepare to establish a Christ-centered home?

Look up this lesson on the Come Follow Me website. Read the opening paragraph and list the important principles there that help you understand what spiritual gifts are and how to use them.

What principles can you find in these sources that are part of a Christ-centered home? In the left column record the principles you find. In the right column record any thoughts you have of specific things the youth can do to prepare for and develop that principle.

Alma 53:20-21	
Alma 56:47-48	
Psalms 127:3	
2 Nephi 25:26	
Mosiah 4:14-15	
D&C 68:25-28	
D&C 88:119	
D&C 93:40	
Ezekiel 16:44	
Family (*For the Strength of Youth*)	
The Family: A Proclamation to the World	

What can you learn from these sources about preparing to establish a Christ-centered home? Make note of special quotes and stories you could use as you are teaching.

- ❖ "To My Grandchildren" by President Henry B. Eyring (October 2013 General Conference)
- ❖ "For Peace at Home" by Elder Richard G. Scott (April 2013 General Conference)
- ❖ "Becoming Goodly Parents" by Elder L. Tom Perry (October 2012 General Conference)

What can I do to help new members of the Church?

Look up this lesson on the Come Follow Me website. Read the opening paragraph and list the important principles there that help you understand the needs of new members of the church and how you can help them.

How do these scriptures apply to you and how can you help new members of the Church?

Luke 22:32	Romans 15:1-2	Moroni 6:4-5
D&C 81:5	D&C 108:7	John 21:15-17

WHAT DOES IT MEAN TO BE A TRUE FRIEND? Look up "Friends" in *For the Strength of Youth* and answer this question.

IDEAS What are some specific ideas you can think of that you could do to help new members of the church?

What do these talks teach you about how you can help new members of the Church? Make note of special quotes and stories you could use as you are teaching.

- ❖ "You Are My Hands" by President Dieter F. Uchtdorf (April 2010 General Conference)
- ❖ "True Friends" by President Henry B. Eyring (April 2002 General Conference)
- ❖ "Helping New Members and Less-Active Members" (*Teaching No Greater Call*, 37)

How can I help my less-active friends return to church?

Look up this lesson on the Come Follow Me website. Read the opening paragraph and list the important principles there that help you understand how you can help your less-active friends.

Read the following parables in **Luke 15** and record how that parable relates to less-active members.

THE LOST SHEEP

THE LOST COIN

THE PRODIGAL SON

What do these scriptures teach you about helping less-active friends?

LUKE 22:32

JOHN 21:15-17

1 PETER 5:2-4

ALMA 31:34-35

D&C 18:10-16

What do these talks teach you about how you can help less-active friends? Make note of special quotes and stories you could use as you are teaching.

- ❖ "Come Join With Us" by President Dieter F. Uchtdorf (October 2013 General Conference)
- ❖ "Waiting for the Prodigal" by Elder Brent H. Nielson (April 2015 General Conference)
- ❖ "Rescue in Unity" by Elder Chi Hong (Sam) Wong (October 2014 General Conference)

What is Zion?

Fill these pages with everything you learn about the following questions. You can use these sources as well as any others you find.

- ❖ "Come to Zion" by Elder D. Todd Christofferson(October 2008 General Conference)
- ❖ "Our Hearts Knit as One" by President Henry B Eyring (October 2008 General Conference)
- ❖ "Sisterhood: Oh, How We Need Each Other" by Sister Bonnie L. Oscarson (April 2014 General Conference)
- ❖ "Zion" *True to the Faith*
- ❖ Mosiah 18:21; D&C 38:26-27; 1 Nephi 13:37; D&C 6:6; 4 Nephi 1:1-18; D&C 97:21; Moses 7:18

What is Zion?

What are people in Zion like?

What do we need to do to bring forth Zion?

What can I do to become a more Zion-like person?

How Can I Participate in the Hastening of the Lord's Work?

Visit www.lds.org and search "hastening the work of salvation". Once you get the search results click on the link that says "Hastening the Work of Salvation: Members and Missionaries" (this website can also be accessed through the "Come Follow Me" web page for this lesson).

Watch some or all of the videos on this page and record your thoughts and feelings here.

_____
_____
_____
_____
_____
_____
_____
_____
_____
_____
_____
_____
_____
_____

What doctrines and principles can you find in these scriptures about hastening the Lord's work?

ISAIAH 11:9   1 NEPHI 13:37   1 NEPHI 14:14

MOSIAH 28:1-3   MOSES 1:39   D&C 138:56

"WANTED: HANDS AND HEARTS TO HASTEN THE WORK" by Sister Linda K. Burton (April 2014 General Conference)

What doctrines and principles can you find in this talk about hastening the Lord's work?

"Here to Serve a Righteous Cause" by Sister Carole F. McConkie (October 2015 General Conference)

What doctrines and principles can you find in this talk about hastening the Lord's work?

How can I learn to serve more effectively in the Church?

Look up this lesson on the Come Follow Me website. Read the opening paragraph and list the important principles there that help you understand how you can learn to serve more effectively in the Church.

Answer the following questions using the suggested scriptures plus any other sources you can find.

How should we act in our callings? Jacob 1:17-19; D&C 4; D&C 107:99; D&C 121:34-36

How are we called to our callings? John 15:16; Article of Faith #5

What can you learn from Emma's calling?

In D&C 25, Emma Smith is given some counsel about fulfilling her responsibilities. Study that section and record any principles you find that would apply to your own responsibilities.

WHAT IF WE FEEL INADEQUATE WHEN CALLED TO A CERTAIN RESPONSIBILITY?

Jeremiah 1:5-9; Mosiah 2:11; Moses 6:31-34

What do these talks teach you about how you can serve more effectively in the Church? Make note of special quotes and stories you could use as you are teaching.

- ❖ "The Savior's Call to Serve" by President Thomas S. Monson (*Ensign*, August 2012, 4-5)
- ❖ "Rise to Your Call" by President Henry B. Eyring (October 2002 General Conference)

How can I become a better leader?

The Lord's Way vs. the World's

What do you observe are some differences between how the Lord would have us lead versus how the world leads?
(Use **Matthew 20:20-28**)

_____

_____

_____

_____

_____

_____

_____

"Leadership in the Church of Jesus Christ"

Read "Leadership in the Church of Jesus Christ" in Handbook 2: Administering the Church (12-14). In the left column record the principles you learn about Christ-like leadership. In the right column, think of a story from the Savior's life when he lived this principle.

What principles can you learn from these scriptures that will help you become a better leader?

Matthew 23:11	D&C 50:26	John 13:4-15	3 Nephi 18:16
3 Nephi 27:21,27	Mosiah 2:11-19	D&C 121:34-36	Exodus 18:13-26

What do these talks teach you about becoming a better leader? Make note of special quotes and stories you could use as you are teaching.

- ❖ "Examples of Righteousness" by President Thomas S. Monson (April 2008 General Conference)
- ❖ "The Power of the Priesthood in the Boy" by Elder Tad R. Callister (April 2013 General Conference)
- ❖ "Leadership in the Church of Jesus Christ," *Handbook 2: Administering in the Church*, 12-14

How can I become a better teacher?

Look up this lesson on the Come Follow Me website. Read the opening paragraph and list the important principles there that help you understand how you can become a better teacher.

What do these scriptures teach you about becoming better teachers?

Ether 12:27

D&C 42:14

D&C 88:78

Teaching the Gospel

Look up "Teaching the Gospel" in *True to the Faith* (168-170). Record any principles and ideas and personal insights that can help you become a better teacher.

Making a Plan to Improve Your Teaching

Look up "Making a Plan to Improve Your Teaching" in *Teaching, No Greater Call* (24-27). Record any principles, ideas and personal insights that can help you become a better teacher.

What do these sources teach you about becoming a better teacher? Make note of special quotes and stories you could use as you are teaching.

- ❖ "Gospel Teaching" by Elder Dallin H. Oaks (October 1999 General Conference)
- ❖ "Teaching with the Power and Authority of God" by David M. McConkie (October 2013 General Conference)
- ❖ "Teaching the Saviors Way" *Teaching the Gospel in the Savior's Way* (link on the Come Follow Me Website)
- ❖ "Teaching the Gospel," *True to the Faith*

What are effective ways to share the gospel with others?

What do these scriptures teach you about sharing the gospel with others?

Matthew 28:19-20

_____

Romans 1:16

_____

1 Timothy 4:12

_____

1 Peter 3:15

_____

D&C 1:23

_____

D&C 11:21

_____

D&C 33:8-10

_____

D&C 88:81

_____

D&C 100:5-8

_____

As you study, fill this box with ideas you have with effective ways you could share the gospel with others.

What do these sources teach you about effective ways to share the gospel with others? Make note of special quotes and stories you could use as you are teaching.

- ❖ "It's a Miracle" by Elder Neil L. Andersen (April 2013 General Conference)
- ❖ "Let the Clarion Trumpet Sound" by Elder Gregory A. Schwitzer (October 2015 General Conference)
- ❖ "Be Thou an Example of the Believers" by Elder Russell M. Nelson (October 2010 General Conference)

Sunday School Curriculum

How can I understand the symbols used to teach about the Second Coming?

The Parable of the Ten Virgins

Study the Parable of the Ten Virgins in **Matthew 25:1-13.** Take each significant detail of the parable and list them in the left column (such as oil, lamp, midnight, the people, etc.) In the right column write what you think those symbols could represent about the Second Coming.

What additional information do these scriptures give you about this parable?

D&C 45:56-57

D&C 63:54

The Parable of the Wheat and the Tares

Study the Parable of the Wheat and the Tares in **Matthew 13:24-30 and D&C 86:1-7.** Take each significant detail of the parable and list them in the left column. In the right column write what you think those symbols could represent about the Second Coming.

The Parable of the Fig Tree

Study the Parable of the Fig Tree in **D&C 45:34-39 and Joseph Smith-Matthew 1:38-39.** Take each significant detail of the parable and list them in the left column. In the right column write what you think those symbols could represent about the Second Coming.

What symbol does the Savior use to describe the Second Coming in these scriptures?

1 THESSALONIANS 5:2-8
2 PETER 3:10-14
D&C 106:4-5
JOSEPH SMITH-MATTHEW 1:46-48

Comparisons and Object Lessons

Look up "Comparisons and Object Lessons" on page 163 of *Teaching No Greater Call.* Why are comparisons and object lessons an effective way of teaching gospel principles?

What does the talk "Preparation for the Second Coming" by Elder Dallin H. Oaks (April 2004 General Conference), teach you about the Second Coming?

What can I learn from the scriptures to help me prepare for the Second Coming?

Look up this lesson on the Come Follow Me website. Read the opening paragraph and list the important principles there that help you understand how you can become a better teacher.

Use the following resources to answer the questions in each box about the Second Coming.

- ❖ "The Second Coming of Jesus Christ," *True to the Faith*, 159-161
- ❖ Luke 21:34-36
- ❖ 2 Peter 3:10-13 (use the Joseph Smith-Translation in the Appendix of your Bible)
- ❖ 1 Nephi 22:17
- ❖ D&C 45:26-44
- ❖ Joseph Smith-Matthew 1:21-40
- ❖ D&C 49:7
- ❖ Joel 2:30-31
- ❖ Matthew 24:29-30
- ❖ D&C 29:14-16
- ❖ Mark 13:32-37

What can I do to prepare?

What will happen?

Christmas: How can I share my testimony that Jesus Christ is the Son of God?

Study the scriptures on this page. Under each section, find at least one principle or part of the story that inspires you to share your testimony of the Savior. Write about it under each section.

Matthew 2

Luke 2

Helaman 14

3 Nephi 1:4-22

28614488R10170

Made in the USA
San Bernardino, CA
02 January 2016